DIGICOMPASS

Sonia Rocca

DIGICOMPASS

Navigating Digital Multiliteracies in Global Language Education

Sonia Rocca
Lycée Français de New York
New York, NY, USA

ISBN 978-3-031-81317-7   ISBN 978-3-031-81318-4 (eBook)
https://doi.org/10.1007/978-3-031-81318-4

© The Editor(s) (if applicable) and The Author(s), under exclusive license to Springer Nature Switzerland AG 2024

This work is subject to copyright. All rights are solely and exclusively licensed by the Publisher, whether the whole or part of the material is concerned, specifically the rights of translation, reprinting, reuse of illustrations, recitation, broadcasting, reproduction on microfilms or in any other physical way, and transmission or information storage and retrieval, electronic adaptation, computer software, or by similar or dissimilar methodology now known or hereafter developed.

The use of general descriptive names, registered names, trademarks, service marks, etc. in this publication does not imply, even in the absence of a specific statement, that such names are exempt from the relevant protective laws and regulations and therefore free for general use.

The publisher, the authors and the editors are safe to assume that the advice and information in this book are believed to be true and accurate at the date of publication. Neither the publisher nor the authors or the editors give a warranty, expressed or implied, with respect to the material contained herein or for any errors or omissions that may have been made. The publisher remains neutral with regard to jurisdictional claims in published maps and institutional affiliations.

This Palgrave Macmillan imprint is published by the registered company Springer Nature Switzerland AG.

The registered company address is: Gewerbestrasse 11, 6330 Cham, Switzerland

If disposing of this product, please recycle the paper.

Alla memoria di papà Mario

"*Non come è morto, ma come viveva*
Non se era ricco - ma quanto lui dava:
Così di una vita il valore va dato
Non certo per quanto contava il casato.
Che importa la chiesa o in cosa credeva -
Chi aveva bisogno accanto lo aveva.
Sempre era pronto a trovare parole
Per far tornare il sorriso e lenire il dolore.
Non quanto e cosa su lui fu detto -
Ma se lo si piange con vero affetto."

—*Anonimo*

Acknowledgments

I wish to express my heartfelt gratitude to the Fulbright Program for granting me the opportunity to serve as a Fulbright Global Scholar and embark on this life-changing journey. To my wonderful hosts in each of the countries I visited, you have not only opened your doors to me but also expanded my horizons. In the order of my travels: the Secondary English Inspectorate in Uruguay, Showa Elementary School attached to Showa Women's University in Japan, and Nazarbayev University Graduate School of Education in Kazakhstan. Your generosity, hospitality, and collaboration made each stop on this journey both meaningful and unforgettable.

My deep appreciation goes to my friend and colleague, Michelle Bedecker, for opening several intellectual doors for me, as well as for providing invaluable feedback and encouragement through her careful and thoughtful reading of the final manuscript.

To my colleagues at the Lycée Français de New York, your dedication, enthusiasm, and passion for education have been a constant source of inspiration. Working alongside you has enriched my life in ways beyond measure.

I would be remiss not to thank the dedicated staff of the Springwater Center for Meditative Inquiry and Retreats in upstate New York for providing a nurturing space that helped me conceive this work.

A special thanks to Cathy Scott, my editor at Palgrave, whose kindness, unwavering support, and insightful guidance have been a beacon throughout this project.

Dulcis in fundo, to my husband, your presence has been my constant comfort and strength. Thank you for your endless encouragement and for being my rock. This journey would not have been possible without you by my side.

New York City
December 2024

Sonia Rocca

Contents

1 Introduction: A Global Approach to Language Education 1

2 DIGICOMPASS: A Framework for Global Language Education 11

3 Theoretical and Technological Foundations of DIGICOMPASS 43

4 Unpacking Digital Literacies and Multiliteracies 73

5 Implementing DIGICOMPASS for the Global Citizen 97

6 AI-XR for Personalized and Experiential Learning in DIGICOMPASS 135

7 Conclusion: Shaping a DIGICOMPASS Future 173

Index 185

List of Figures

Fig. 2.1	Features of global language education in DIGICOMPASS	20
Fig. 2.2	Data-driven personalization in adaptive learning	29
Fig. 3.1	DIGICOMPASS theoretical foundations	46
Fig. 3.2	Technological intersection and compatibility	65
Fig. 6.1	Personalized and experiential learning in DIGICOMPASS	137
Fig. 7.1	DIGICOMPASS in a Global Classroom (as conceptualized by ChatGPT 4.0)	174
Fig. 7.2	Teaching 2.0 in the age of emerging technologies	178

List of Tables

Table 3.1	Adaptive learning technologies in DIGICOMPASS	47
Table 3.2	Assistive technologies in DIGICOMPASS	48
Table 3.3	Immersive technologies in DIGICOMPASS	49
Table 3.4	Collaborative technologies in DIGICOMPASS	49
Table 3.5	Data analytic technologies in DIGICOMPASS	50
Table 3.6	Content delivery technologies in DIGICOMPASS	51
Table 3.7	Gamification technologies in DIGICOMPASS	51
Table 3.8	Intersecting technologies in DIGICOMPASS	62
Table 4.1	Spectrum of digital multiliteracies in DIGICOMPASS	82
Table 5.1	DIGICOMPASS mapping with IB curriculum: Year 7 to Year 12 progression	102
Table 5.2	UN SDGs and DIGICOMPASS alignment	103
Table 5.3	CEFR and DIGICOMPASS alignment	106
Table 5.4	DIGICOMPASS strategic implementation and scalability	112
Table 5.5	Feedback loop and personalized learning in DIGICOMPASS	119
Table 6.1	Weeks 1–2 lesson plan: introduction to climate change and environmental science	164

CHAPTER 1

Introduction: A Global Approach to Language Education

Abstract This introductory chapter presents the DIGICOMPASS framework, emphasizing its holistic, interdisciplinary, and modular design. It redefines global language education not as the teaching of widely spoken "global" languages but as language education that is inherently global, recognizing all languages as essential connectors across cultural and geographical divides. Targeted at secondary education, DIGICOMPASS integrates global citizenship into language education, equipping students with the knowledge, skills, and empathy to address complex global challenges. The framework prioritizes personalized and immersive learning experiences, focusing on digital literacy, intercultural competence, and interdisciplinary collaboration. Additionally, it addresses critical implementation challenges, including digital equity and cultural relevance. By bridging established pedagogies with emerging technologies, DIGICOMPASS provides a roadmap for fostering inclusive and forward-thinking education in an increasingly interconnected world.

Keywords Adaptive learning • Emergent technologies • Global citizenship • Global language education • Interconnectedness

In a world where borders blur and cultures converge, the language we speak is only the beginning. As technology and education intersect and reshape the way we learn, the future of language education must extend beyond traditional methods. Global language education, as used in this context, refers not to the teaching of languages that are considered "global" or widely spoken, but rather to the idea that all languages are global. Every language has the potential to connect individuals across cultural and geographical boundaries, making each one an essential part of our global tapestry.

This perspective rejects the notion of any language being "foreign." The term "foreign" sets up unnecessary barriers and reinforces outdated concepts of linguistic hierarchies. In this volume, we consciously avoid using the term "foreign" because it perpetuates the idea that some languages are distant or disconnected from our shared human experience. Instead, we embrace the view that all languages contribute to global understanding and that learning any language is an act of engaging with the world in a meaningful way.

1.1 The Urgency of Global Citizenship

The true challenge of our time lies in understanding, empathizing, and connecting across invisible divides. Today, global citizenship has evolved from a theoretical ideal to an educational imperative. Global citizens are individuals equipped with the knowledge, skills, and attitudes necessary to engage with the world in an informed, empathetic, and responsible manner. They are prepared to tackle complex global challenges—such as climate change, social inequality, and cultural conflicts—through collaboration, innovation, and ethical leadership.

DIGICOMPASS places global citizenship at the core of its educational philosophy, recognizing that language is not merely a means of communication but a vital tool for building knowledge, as well as cultivating intercultural understanding, empathy, and cooperation. By embedding global citizenship into the fabric of language education, DIGICOMPASS ensures that students become proficient in multiple languages and adept at navigating the cultural and ethical dimensions of our global society.

1.2 Harmonizing for Holism: The DIGICOMPASS Framework

DIGICOMPASS transcends traditional language learning objectives by offering a holistic, multidimensional, interdisciplinary, and modular framework designed to meet the complex demands of global language education. By harmonizing adaptive learning technologies, digital multiliteracies, and interdisciplinary approaches, DIGICOMPASS ensures that education is both comprehensive and adaptable, responding effectively to the evolving needs of students in a rapidly globalizing world.

- *Holistic and Multidimensional:* At the core of DIGICOMPASS is the belief that effective language education must address the whole student, integrating linguistic abilities with digital literacy, intercultural competence, and global citizenship. This holistic approach considers all aspects of the learning experience, ensuring that students develop not only academically but also as culturally aware and socially responsible individuals. The multidimensional nature of DIGICOMPASS allows it to address these diverse aspects of education simultaneously, creating a rich and nuanced learning environment.
- *Interdisciplinary:* DIGICOMPASS breaks down traditional academic silos, encouraging interdisciplinary learning that connects language education with various fields such as technology, science, culture, and social studies. This interdisciplinary approach fosters a deeper understanding of how language interacts with different areas of knowledge, promoting a comprehensive perspective that is essential in today's interconnected world.
- *Modular:* The modular design of DIGICOMPASS allows for flexible and customizable learning pathways, tailored to the unique needs, abilities, and modalities of each student. This flexibility enables educators to adapt the framework to different curricula, ensuring that learning is contextually relevant to local educational goals and cultural contexts. The modular structure also supports continuous learning, allowing students to build on their knowledge incrementally and at their own pace.

> Key Elements of the DIGICOMPASS Framework
>
> - *Cultural and Linguistic Understanding:* Encouraging immersion in cultural contexts to appreciate nuances and perspectives, fostering a deep understanding of diverse ways of life.
> - *Interconnectedness Across Languages:* Promoting the learning of multiple languages and highlighting the interconnectedness of global cultures, enriching students' worldviews.
> - *Knowledge Construction:* Utilizing language as a medium to develop critical thinking and problem-solving skills, equipping students for active participation in a globally interconnected community.
> - *Real-World Application:* Incorporating experiential learning through international collaborations and real-world practice, allowing students to apply their language skills in diverse contexts.
> - *Global Citizenship:* Cultivating globally aware citizens who are culturally sensitive and ethically responsible, prepared to engage meaningfully in a rapidly changing world.

This integrated, learner-centered approach enhances linguistic proficiency while fostering both academic excellence and personal growth, establishing DIGICOMPASS as a comprehensive framework for global language education, specifically tailored for secondary education. This book is designed with a diverse range of stakeholders in mind, each of whom plays a crucial role in the successful implementation of DIGICOMPASS:

- TEACHERS will access advanced tools for personalizing learning, ensuring diverse student needs are met in Global Classroom settings. The framework also offers professional development in emerging technologies like artificial intelligence (AI) and extended reality (XR), enhancing teachers' role as innovative educators.
- CURRICULUM DEVELOPERS will benefit from DIGICOMPASS's flexible, modular structure, which integrates digital literacies, intercultural competence, and interdisciplinary connections into engaging curricula suited for the digital age.

- ADMINISTRATORS will find strategic insights in DIGICOMPASS for updating curricula, resource allocation, and program evaluation, ensuring inclusive and technologically enhanced educational environments.
- POLICYMAKERS will gain strategies for integrating technology into language education while ensuring equitable access. DIGICOMPASS supports long-term planning and policies that promote global citizenship and digital literacy.
- PARENTS will be informed on how DIGICOMPASS supports their children's academic and personal growth, enabling them to actively participate in fostering digital literacy and cultural awareness at home.
- STUDENTS will experience personalized learning that develops critical global competencies like digital literacy and intercultural communication, preparing them for success in a globalized, digital world.

1.3 The Role of Emergent Technologies

Emergent technologies are transforming language education by creating dynamic, immersive, and personalized learning experiences, central to the DIGICOMPASS framework. At its heart is personalized learning, enabled by adaptive technologies that tailor education to each student's needs. Digital literacy serves as the guiding north of this metaphorical compass, making cutting-edge technology essential for the framework's success. To achieve these goals, several key technologies are integral to the DIGICOMPASS framework:

- *Artificial Intelligence (AI):* AI-powered tools provide personalized learning pathways by adapting to individual student needs and offering real-time feedback. AI enhances the learning process by analyzing performance and adjusting content delivery to optimize understanding and retention. It also manages cognitive load, ensuring students are neither overwhelmed nor under-stimulated, and anticipates student needs to adjust learning pathways accordingly.
- *Extended Reality (XR):* XR, including virtual reality (VR), augmented reality (AR), and mixed reality (MR), creates immersive environments where students engage in simulated real-world scenarios. XR enhances comprehension of complex concepts and fosters intercultural competence by providing rich, immersive cultural

experiences, making language immersion more effective and contextually relevant.
- *Adaptive Learning Technologies:* These technologies use data analytics to personalize learning experiences, ensuring content meets the unique needs and pace of each student. They are central to DIGICOMPASS, creating a responsive learning environment where each student's journey is continuously refined based on evolving performance metrics. Real-time feedback systems support continuous improvement in student outcomes.
- *Gamification:* Integrating game elements into education motivates students by making learning interactive and enjoyable. Gamification strategies, such as earning points and completing challenges, increase engagement and persistence. In DIGICOMPASS, gamification not only motivates but also supports deeper cognitive engagement by framing educational content within rewarding, challenging contexts.
- *Collaboration:* Digital platforms that facilitate collaboration among students and educators globally are essential for language education. These platforms enable real-time communication, group projects, and resource sharing, helping students build intercultural competencies. Collaborative features support plurilingualism, allowing for authentic language practice in diverse, interactive settings, while creating a Global Classroom that is both inclusive and culturally enriching.

1.4 Scope, Objectives, and Challenges

DIGICOMPASS is designed to create a comprehensive and inclusive framework for global language education by harmonizing learning practices, promoting interdisciplinary connections, and enhancing accessibility for all learners. By integrating adaptive learning technologies and digital multiliteracies, DIGICOMPASS offers a personalized, student-centered approach to education that prepares students to navigate the digital world and become culturally aware global citizens. The framework encourages the breakdown of traditional subject boundaries, enabling the application of language skills across various disciplines and deepening the understanding of the intersections between language, culture, technology, and global issues. Furthermore, DIGICOMPASS emphasizes equity, ensuring that educational opportunities are accessible to all students, regardless of their socioeconomic background or starting level.

While the DIGICOMPASS framework offers a promising model for integrating technology and intercultural learning, its implementation poses several significant challenges. One of the primary obstacles is harmonizing emergent technologies, such as AI and XR, with traditional educational practices. It is crucial to find ways to integrate these innovations without disrupting established pedagogical approaches. Striking the right balance between technological advancements and conventional teaching practices will not only enhance language proficiency but also foster cultural competence among students.

Another major challenge involves ensuring accessibility and digital equity. As technologies like AI and XR become more central to education, it is essential to make them available to all learners, especially those in under-resourced areas. Addressing the disparities in access to devices, Internet connectivity, and digital training for both educators and students is vital for equitable implementation. Without such strategies, the full potential of DIGICOMPASS could be out of reach for many students, perpetuating existing educational inequalities.

Finally, customizing learning experiences to meet the diverse needs of students is critical for the successful application of DIGICOMPASS. The framework must be adaptable to various educational contexts, cultural backgrounds, and learning profiles. This requires the development of tailored approaches that respect and incorporate local languages, cultures, and educational traditions while still maintaining the global perspective central to DIGICOMPASS. Balancing this local-global dynamic is key to ensuring that the framework is both relevant and effective across a range of learning environments.

These challenges are acknowledged as part of the ongoing development of DIGICOMPASS. While this publication outlines the core principles and concepts of the framework, we recognize that more work is needed to address the complexities of implementing DIGICOMPASS in diverse contexts. This first publication provides a foundational understanding and introduces practical strategies for educators, administrators, and policymakers. However, it does not fully explore all potential challenges and adaptations necessary for widespread implementation. We plan to explore these challenges further in subsequent publications. Future work will delve deeper into:

- CASE STUDIES AND REAL-WORLD APPLICATIONS: Detailed examples from various cultural, geographical, and socioeconomic contexts will

be provided to illustrate how DIGICOMPASS can be adapted and applied effectively.
- DIGITAL EQUITY AND ETHICAL CONSIDERATIONS: Follow-up studies will investigate strategies for overcoming barriers to technology access and usage, with a focus on ethical implications and digital inclusion.
- TEACHER EDUCATION AND PROFESSIONAL DEVELOPMENT: Future publications will outline comprehensive strategies for integrating DIGICOMPASS into teacher education programs, providing training modules and assessment tools to help educators implement this framework effectively.

By continuously refining and expanding on the DIGICOMPASS framework, we aim to provide a robust roadmap for creating innovative, inclusive, and context-sensitive educational environments that equip students with the linguistic and intercultural competencies needed to thrive in a globalized, digital world.

1.5 STRUCTURE OF THE VOLUME

In addition to this introductory chapter, which sets the stage and provides a general overview of the key themes and concepts, this volume is organized into seven chapters, each addressing specific aspects of the DIGICOMPASS framework.

Chapter 2, "DIGICOMPASS: A Framework for Global Language Education," introduces the core principles and concepts that form the foundation of the framework. Chapter 3, "Theoretical and Technological Foundations of DIGICOMPASS," delves into the pedagogical theories and technological innovations that underpin the framework's design and application. In Chap. 4, "Unpacking Digital Literacies and Multiliteracies," the expanding role of digital literacies in education is explored, particularly in the context of multilingual and multicultural learning environments.

Chapter 5, "Implementing DIGICOMPASS for the Global Citizen," offers strategies for integrating DIGICOMPASS into existing curricula and emphasizes the promotion of global citizenship through education. Chapter 6, "AI-XR for Personalized and Experiential Learning in DIGICOMPASS," examines the role of artificial intelligence (AI) and extended reality (XR) in creating personalized and immersive learning experiences. Finally, Chap. 7, "Shaping a DIGICOMPASS Future," synthesizes the insights from the previous chapters and presents a vision for the future of global language education, highlighting the potential evolution of the DIGICOMPASS framework.

DIGICOMPASS serves both as a metaphor and as a symbol within the realm of global language education. As a metaphor, DIGICOMPASS likens the educational framework to a physical compass, guiding students and educators through the complex terrain of contemporary education. Just as a compass provides direction and helps navigate uncharted territories, DIGICOMPASS steers students toward a comprehensive and personalized learning experience, ensuring they acquire not only knowledge but also the skills necessary to thrive in an interconnected, digital world. This metaphor underscores the role of DIGICOMPASS in offering clarity and focus amidst the vast array of educational challenges and opportunities.

As a symbol, DIGICOMPASS represents the broader ideals of global citizenship, intercultural understanding, and digital literacy. It stands for the integration of advanced technologies, personalized learning, and ethical engagement as core components of twenty-first-century education. Symbolically, DIGICOMPASS embodies the direction and purpose that contemporary education must embrace to prepare students for the complexities of global society. It signifies a commitment to navigating the digital age with a deep sense of responsibility and global awareness.

In essence, while the metaphor of DIGICOMPASS illustrates its function as a conceptual tool in education, the symbol encapsulates its mission—equipping learners with the knowledge, skills, and values needed to contribute meaningfully to the world. With this understanding of DIGICOMPASS as both a guiding metaphor and a powerful symbol, the next chapter delves into the core principles and concepts that form the foundation of this novel educational framework.

CHAPTER 2

DIGICOMPASS: A Framework for Global Language Education

Abstract DIGICOMPASS integrates its four core principles—digital literacy, inclusive practices, intercultural competence, and awareness of social strategies—into global citizenship, the central focus of the framework. With an emphasis on global language education, it incorporates plurilingualism and key features such as intercultural competence, linguistic, sociolinguistic, and pragmatic competencies, as well as mediation strategies. These elements align with the Common European Framework of Reference for Languages (CEFR) principles to promote adaptable language use in diverse contexts. Inclusive practices prioritize equity and accessibility, fostering a sense of belonging and ensuring that diverse learner needs are met. Additionally, DIGICOMPASS harnesses AI-driven adaptive learning technologies to enhance multiliteracies, providing personalized and equitable education. By fostering ethical engagement and sustainability, DIGICOMPASS prepares learners to address global challenges with responsibility and equity.

Keywords Digital literacy • Inclusive practices • Intercultural competence • Plurilingualism • Social responsibility

2.1 Introduction

Welcome to DIGICOMPASS,[1] a symbolic compass designed to navigate the complexities of contemporary education. Centered around global citizenship, DIGICOMPASS directs learning through four cardinal points, each representing a core principle essential for nurturing globally aware and socially responsible individuals:

- Digital Literacy (North): Serving as our guiding star, it equips students with the skills to safely and healthily navigate, critically evaluate, and competently contribute to the digital world.
- Inclusive Practices (East): Reflecting an educational sunrise, it promotes equality, inclusivity, and a sense of belonging, fostering an environment where every student feels valued and supported.
- Intercultural Competence (South): Embracing the rich tapestry of human experience, it celebrates cultural diversity, nurturing understanding, empathy, and respect for the myriad ways people express their identities.
- Awareness of Social Strategies (West): Symbolizing twilight reflection, it encourages contemplation on societal impacts, emphasizing ethical engagement and sustainable development while promoting community growth.

The core principles of DIGICOMPASS are interwoven within a modular framework, ensuring they are integrated and strengthened across various contexts. This approach promotes holistic understanding and practical application. The following sections will explore each principle in detail, demonstrating their collective contribution to the overarching goals of DIGICOMPASS.

---

[1] A preliminary overview of DIGICOMPASS was presented at the 14th International Conference "The Future of Education" (Rocca, 2024).

2.2 DIGICOMPASS Core Principles

DIGICOMPASS presents a synergistic integration of digital literacy, inclusive practices, intercultural competence, and awareness of social strategies—fundamental elements that collectively forge the framework's foundational acronym: Digital, Inclusive, Global Intercultural Competence, Awareness of Social Strategies.

2.2.1 Digital Literacy

DIGICOMPASS's educational ethos is deeply rooted in nurturing digital literacy—the guiding north of our metaphorical compass—as a multiliteracy (see Chap. 4), elevating the concept beyond mere technological fluency, encompassing a broad set of capabilities required to effectively navigate, evaluate, and create information using various digital technologies. According to Eshet-Alkalai (2004), these skills include photo-visual literacy (understanding and interpreting visual information), reproduction literacy (creating new content by remixing existing materials), branching literacy (navigating non-linear, hypertextual information structures), information literacy (critically evaluating the credibility and relevance of information), and socio-emotional literacy (engaging ethically and responsibly in digital communities).

Within DIGICOMPASS, digital literacy is approached as an engaged, participatory practice where learners are not just consumers of digital content but also active contributors. Jenkins et al. (2016) emphasize the role of learners as protagonists in the digital landscape, actively shaping and being shaped by the cultural narratives they engage with. Digital storytelling is a powerful educational tool that integrates multiple literacies, allowing students to express themselves creatively while developing essential digital skills. Chan et al. (2017) describe digital storytelling as the process of combining text, images, audio, and video to create compelling narratives. This process fosters creative expression, encourages students to tell their stories in engaging and imaginative ways, and develops technical skills for media creation and editing. It also enhances narrative competence, enabling students to structure and convey stories effectively. In the context of DIGICOMPASS, digital storytelling serves as a vehicle for embodying various literacies, providing a platform for students to explore and articulate their ideas, reflect on their experiences, and connect with broader cultural and social issues. By engaging in digital storytelling, students enhance their media literacy, critical thinking, and communication skills, all crucial for navigating the digital world.

Eshet-Alkalai (2004) expands on the concept of digital literacy by presenting it as a multifaceted framework encompassing various survival skills necessary in the digital era. Integrating these elements, DIGICOMPASS ensures that students are proficient in using digital tools and capable of critically engaging with digital content and participating ethically in digital communities. Tinmaz et al. (2022) highlight the importance of these competencies, noting that a systematic approach to digital literacy significantly improves students' ability to critically assess and create digital content, leading to more informed and engaged digital citizens.

Importantly, digital literacy is intrinsically linked to the concept of global citizenship. This connection ensures that students not only consume digital content but also critically evaluate and produce content that reflects their understanding of global contexts. UNESCO (2018) underscores the global importance of digital literacy skills, providing a framework that supports sustainable development by equipping learners with essential digital competencies. Digitally literate students are prepared to engage with global issues, participate in international dialogues, and contribute meaningfully to a global community. Greenhow et al. (2019) emphasize the significant role of social media in education, discussing how it can enhance learning experiences by fostering interaction and engagement, providing new platforms for collaboration, and reshaping traditional educational boundaries.

2.2.2 Inclusive Practices

As DIGICOMPASS moves toward a digital literacy-focused pedagogy that encourages creative and ethical engagement with media, it also lays a critical foundation for embracing the full spectrum of student diversity. By fostering digital authorship, where learners shape their own narratives, DIGICOMPASS creates a bridge to personalized learning experiences. These experiences are grounded in research-informed strategies such as differentiated instruction, personalized learning, and adaptive learning.

Inclusive practices are essential for creating a supportive learning environment where all students feel valued and empowered. Inclusivity in education means recognizing and addressing the diverse needs of students, providing equitable opportunities for learning, and fostering a sense of belonging. DIGICOMPASS is committed to implementing inclusive practices that ensure every student can thrive academically and personally.

Differentiated instruction involves tailoring educational experiences to meet the diverse needs of students. According to Tomlinson and Imbeau (2023), this approach addresses students' varying readiness levels, interests, and learning profiles, providing multiple paths to learning. DIGICOMPASS supports differentiated instruction to ensure that every student's unique needs are met within the classroom. Recent studies, such as those by AM et al. (2023), demonstrate that differentiated instruction can significantly enhance student engagement and learning outcomes. Moreover, research by Gibbs (2022) highlights the challenges and strategies for effectively implementing differentiated instruction in secondary schools, emphasizing the importance of teacher training, resource allocation, and ongoing support to overcome obstacles in applying differentiation effectively.

Personalized learning goes beyond differentiated instruction by tailoring the entire educational experience to each student's unique abilities and needs. Hattie (2012) emphasizes the significance of personalized learning in improving student outcomes by allowing students to learn at their own pace and according to their interests. DIGICOMPASS embraces personalized learning by creating educational experiences that cater to the distinct abilities and needs of each student. Similarly, Deunk et al. (2018) highlight how personalized learning pathways increase student motivation and academic performance.

Integrating both differentiated instruction and personalized learning is complemented by adaptive learning technologies, which use real-time data to dynamically adjust the learning experience based on student performance. Walkington and Bernacki (2020) illustrate how adaptive learning technologies enhance student engagement and achievement by providing customized educational experiences that respond to the learner's current understanding and progress. DIGICOMPASS integrates adaptive learning technologies to ensure that each student receives the support and challenges they need to succeed. Furthermore, a study by Gligorea et al. (2023) confirms the efficacy of adaptive learning systems in providing individualized instruction that leads to improved student achievements.

Thus, DIGICOMPASS not only equips students to navigate the digital landscape but also commits to inclusive practices that value and respond to their diverse educational needs. To achieve this, DIGICOMPASS supports culturally responsive education to honor students' cultural backgrounds and integrate diverse perspectives into the curriculum. Gay (2018) discusses how this approach validates and reflects the diverse cultural backgrounds of students, promoting higher engagement and academic success. Her research underscores the need for teachers to recognize and respect cultural differences, a core principle of the DIGICOMPASS framework. Moreover, Reimers's (2020) exploration of education's role in addressing sustainability and inequality further advances this global perspective, arguing for preparing students to tackle global issues and fostering a sense of responsibility and agency. Yoon (2023) and Harkins Monaco et al. (2023) provide updated insights into the implementation of culturally and linguistically responsive teaching, which align with the inclusive practices that DIGICOMPASS aims to promote.

While culturally responsive teaching focuses on honoring and integrating students' cultural backgrounds, Universal Design for Learning (UDL) emphasizes creating flexible learning environments that accommodate diverse learning needs. Both approaches aim to make education more inclusive and accessible. UDL principles further support the inclusive ethos of DIGICOMPASS by ensuring that all students can access and engage with the curriculum in ways that work best for them. CAST (2024) details how UDL provides multiple means of representation to give learners various ways to acquire information and knowledge, multiple means of action and expression to provide learners alternatives for demonstrating what they know, and multiple means of engagement to tap into learners' interests, challenge them appropriately, and motivate them to learn.

Nurturing an inclusive educational environment requires addressing students' overall well-being and social-emotional development. Cipriano and McCarthy (2023) highlight the importance of social-emotional learning (SEL) in creating inclusive educational settings, while Schwartz et al. (2023) emphasize integrating SEL within academic instruction to promote transformative learning experiences. Incorporating SEL into the DIGICOMPASS framework ensures students are both academically successful and emotionally competent. SEL helps students develop self-awareness, self-management, social awareness, relationship skills, and responsible decision-making. DIGICOMPASS supports SEL through activities like classroom discussions, role-playing scenarios, and group projects that promote empathy and effective communication.

Inclusive practices within the DIGICOMPASS framework are intricately woven together to create a seamless and supportive educational environment. Adaptivity ensures that learning experiences can be tailored in real-time to meet students' evolving needs, while personalization focuses on customizing the entire educational journey based on individual preferences. Differentiation provides varied pathways for learning, accommodating diverse readiness levels, interests, and learning profiles. Culturally responsive education honors and integrates students' cultural backgrounds, and Universal Design for Learning (UDL) ensures accessibility through multiple means of representation, engagement, and expression. Social-emotional learning (SEL) cultivates essential life skills such as empathy, self-management, and responsible decision-making. Together, these inclusive practices foster another DIGICOMPASS cardinal pillar, that is, intercultural competence, preparing students to thrive in a diverse and interconnected world.

2.2.3   Intercultural Competence

Recognizing its pivotal role in shaping global citizens, DIGICOMPASS builds on Byram's (2020) foundational work on intercultural competence, which lays the groundwork for understanding the knowledge, skills, and attitudes necessary for effective intercultural communication. Byram's framework consists of five key components: attitudes (openness and curiosity), knowledge (of social groups and their practices), skills of interpreting and relating, skills of discovery and interaction, and critical cultural awareness. These elements are foundational to DIGICOMPASS as they help students develop the ability to navigate cultural differences and engage respectfully with diverse perspectives. Jackson (2019) expands on these concepts by exploring intercultural competence in contemporary global contexts, emphasizing the need for adaptability and continuous learning. This insight helps DIGICOMPASS prepare students for real-world interactions by fostering flexibility and a commitment to ongoing intercultural learning. Because intercultural competence should not only be taught but also experienced and internalized, DIGICOMPASS draws on Deardorff's (2020) strategies for integrating intercultural competence in the curriculum, such as creating immersive intercultural experiences and promoting critical reflection on cultural interactions. Moreover, DIGICOMPASS draws on Bennett's (2013) Developmental Model of Intercultural Sensitivity (DMIS) to guide students through their intercultural learning journey, helping them progress from ethnocentric stages to more ethnorelative stages of understanding. This is achieved through structured activities that challenge students to reflect on their own cultural biases and develop a deeper appreciation for cultural diversity.

To further enhance this goal, DIGICOMPASS incorporates practical strategies from Spitzberg and Changnon (2009), such as active listening, perspective-taking, and conflict resolution. In a similar vein, Gee (2015) focuses on the role of discourse in intercultural communication, stressing the importance of language and social practices in shaping cultural understanding. DIGICOMPASS integrates Gee's insights using activities and discussions that enhance students' language proficiency and their ability to engage in meaningful cross-cultural dialogues. These strategies are enriched by aligning with the Common European Framework of Reference for Languages (CEFR, Council of Europe, 2001, 2020), which outlines detailed descriptors of language competence essential for intercultural communication. CEFR 2020 expands on the ability to mediate across languages and cultures, reflecting an evolved understanding of language learning's role in developing intercultural competence.

2.2.4 Awareness of Social Strategies

By bridging the comprehensive focus on intercultural competence with the framework's broader societal objectives, DIGICOMPASS equips students for effective cross-cultural communication and fosters a deeper engagement with social strategies. This seamless transition underscores the framework's holistic approach, linking the mastery of cultural nuances and intercultural dialogue to a nuanced understanding of social dynamics. Social strategies, which are techniques and approaches used to navigate and influence social interactions effectively, are significant because they enable individuals to engage ethically and responsibly within their communities, fostering social cohesion and promoting positive societal change. Integrating an awareness of social strategies, DIGICOMPASS prepares learners for navigating cultural diversity and sensitizes them to the societal implications of their actions and interactions.

This awareness is key to understanding how individuals and communities can drive social change and is deeply connected to the framework's commitment to social responsibility. It instills in learners the ability to apply their knowledge and skills in ways that contribute positively to society, a principle that resonates with Shulman's (2005) advocacy for education to foster ethical and responsible action. DIGICOMPASS intertwines this awareness with actionable steps toward social responsibility, encouraging students not only to reflect on societal issues but also to become agents of change. This alignment with Schön's (2010) reflective practice and Bornstein's (2007) focus on social entrepreneurship illustrates the transformative power of education in nurturing innovators and leaders who can address social challenges.

DIGICOMPASS incorporates awareness of social strategies to ensure students are not only knowledgeable but also capable of ethical action. By engaging in reflective practices, such as journaling and group discussions on social issues, students cultivate critical thinking skills and a sense of social responsibility. Schön's (2010) concept of reflective practice encourages students to reflect on their experiences and societal issues, enabling them to critically evaluate their actions and the impact they have on their communities, thus promoting a cycle of continuous improvement and ethical engagement.

Bornstein (2007) highlights the role of social entrepreneurship in driving social change. DIGICOMPASS integrates this perspective by encouraging students to develop innovative solutions to societal problems. Through project-based learning and community engagement activities, students learn to identify issues, develop strategies, and implement projects that address these challenges. This hands-on approach not only enhances their learning but also empowers them to become proactive agents of change. Zhao (2018) discusses the importance of fostering global competence and social responsibility in education. Similarly, Rieckmann (2018) emphasizes the need for education systems to develop students' capabilities to contribute to sustainable development, reinforcing the importance of integrating social responsibility into the curriculum. These insights highlight the evolving educational landscape and the necessity for frameworks like DIGICOMPASS to adapt and respond to these global imperatives.

In sum, DIGICOMPASS embodies a synergistic integration of four core principles, represented as the cardinal points of a metaphorical compass, all converging toward the core of digital citizenship. Digital literacy in the North acts as the guiding star; inclusive practices in the East reflect the dawn of a new educational approach; intercultural competence in the South embraces the rich tapestry of human experience; awareness of social strategies in the West symbolizes twilight reflection. In the next section, we will explore the critical role of plurilingualism and global language education in shaping global citizenship, highlighting the vital importance of language education with a global dimension.

2.3 Embracing Plurilingualism and Global Language Education

Adhering to the principles of CEFR 2020, DIGICOMPASS emphasizes nurturing plurilingual and interculturally competent global citizens. This approach to global language education focuses on developing linguistic and cultural competencies that enable students to communicate and interact effectively across multiple languages and cultural contexts. A global dimension is integral to this framework, stressing active participation in an interconnected world and fostering the ability to contribute positively to global society (Council of Europe, 2020). As illustrated in Fig. 2.1, DIGICOMPASS identifies eight key features of global language education: intercultural competence, plurilingualism, linguistic competence, sociolinguistic competence, pragmatic competence, mediation strategies, digital literacy, and global citizenship. These features emphasize cultivating cultural awareness, promoting inclusivity, mastering language use in

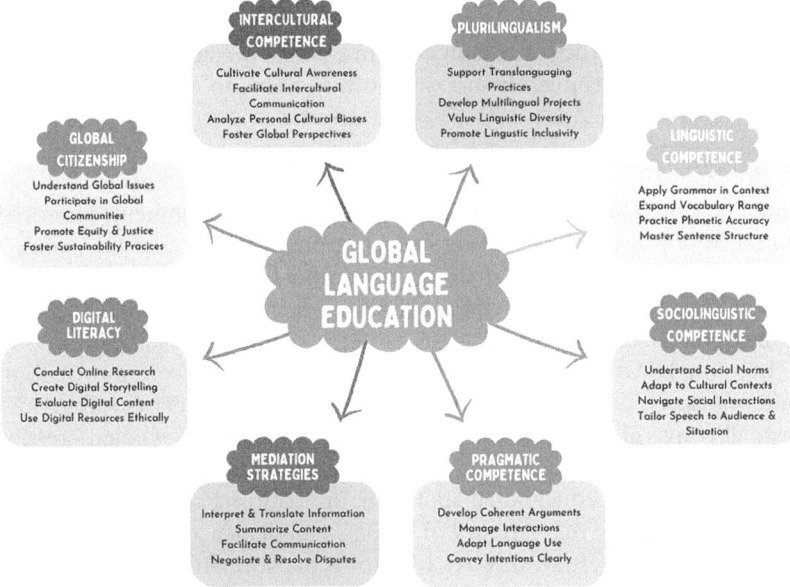

Fig. 2.1 Features of global language education in DIGICOMPASS

context, and fostering equity and sustainability. Together, they support the development of adaptable and practical language proficiency essential for diverse societal contexts.

The ethos of the DIGICOMPASS approach resonates with the work of Coste et al. (2009), promoting an appreciation of cultural diversity and preparing learners to adeptly navigate the intricacies of global, multicultural environments. The integration of multiple languages aligns with contemporary research that underscores the advantages of such inclusivity. The adoption of Content and Language Integrated Learning (CLIL), as highlighted by Coyle et al. (2010), plays a crucial role in combining language learning with content instruction, enhancing both linguistic proficiency and critical cultural understanding. Llinares and Cross (2022) underscore significant challenges and equity issues in the implementation of CLIL, noting that while CLIL can enhance language proficiency and content knowledge, it may also exacerbate inequalities if not carefully adapted to local contexts and diverse student needs. They advocate for updated pedagogical strategies and targeted professional development to address these equity concerns, ensuring that all students, regardless of socio-economic or cultural background, can benefit from CLIL. DIGICOMPASS aligns with these insights by embedding inclusive practices as a core principle (see Sect. 2.2.2), promoting equitable education that fosters both linguistic proficiency and academic success.

Additionally, DIGICOMPASS's plurilingual approach significantly enhances intercultural competence. Drawing on Byram's (2020) principles, it prepares students to navigate cultural boundaries with sensitivity and skill, recognizing that effective intercultural communication requires a deep awareness and appreciation of linguistic and cultural nuances. The symbiotic relationship between language and culture, as articulated by Kramsch (1993), is foundational to the framework's philosophy. Kramsch emphasized that language learning is deeply embedded within its cultural context, asserting that true language competence requires understanding cultural nuances and social practices. Building on this foundation, Jackson (2019) and Deardorff (2020) provide practical strategies for integrating intercultural competence into language education. Jackson highlights the necessity of intercultural communicative competence in our globalized world, offering strategies to help learners navigate and appreciate cultural differences. Similarly, Deardorff's Story Circles promotes intercultural understanding through guided storytelling and reflective dialogue, aligning with the emphasis on the interplay between language and culture.

Intercultural communication and competence are intrinsically linked within the DIGICOMPASS framework. Communication in this context refers to the actual exchange of ideas and information across cultures, while competence refers to the learner's ability to do so effectively and appropriately. Such competence is cultivated through experiences and education that foster the ability to navigate intercultural differences, leading to effective communication. Intercultural competence involves the ability to understand and engage with cultural diversity, facilitating mutual respect and social cohesion. Defined by Beacco et al. (2016) as "the ability to experience otherness and cultural diversity" (p. 10), intercultural competence encompasses a wide range of skills and knowledge that enable individuals to navigate different cultural settings effectively. Plurilingualism is essential in this context because it allows individuals to draw on their entire linguistic and cultural repertoire, enhancing their ability to interact meaningfully across diverse cultural contexts.

The concept of intercultural awareness, as initially described in the CEFR 2001, focuses on understanding the relationship between one's own culture and the target culture (Council of Europe, 2001, p. 103). It includes the development of intercultural skills and know-how, such as bridging cultural differences, acting as an intermediary, and demonstrating cultural sensitivity. These skills are crucial for effective communication and interaction in a multicultural world. Beacco et al. (2016) expand on these concepts by advocating for a comprehensive approach to intercultural competence. This guide highlights the importance of linguistic diversity and intercultural understanding in fostering mutual respect and social cohesion. It emphasizes the development of competencies beyond traditional language skills, including cultural awareness, critical thinking, and reflexivity. Reflexivity, or the ability to reflect critically on one's own cultural assumptions and those of others, is a key component of intercultural competence. The integration of plurilingual and intercultural education across all subject areas ensures that intercultural competence becomes a foundational aspect of the entire educational experience.

CEFR 2020 further elaborates on intercultural competence, linking it with plurilingual and pluricultural competence, sociolinguistic competence, and pragmatic competence, as well as mediation activities and strategies. Plurilingual and pluricultural competence involves using one's entire linguistic and cultural repertoire to communicate effectively, promoting both language learning and cultural awareness (Council of Europe, 2020). This competence encourages learners to draw on their knowledge of multiple languages and cultures to enhance communication and understanding, thereby fostering a deeper connection between language and cultural identity.

Sociolinguistic competence involves understanding and using language appropriately in various social contexts. It considers factors such as social norms, cultural conventions, and context-specific language use, which are crucial for effective intercultural communication (Byram, 2020). Pragmatic competence encompasses skills such as organizing discourse, using language functions effectively, and managing interactions to achieve communicative goals. These competencies enable learners to navigate the complexities of social interactions in a multicultural environment (Taguchi, 2011).

Intercultural competence is also pivotal in mediation activities and strategies. These activities, which include translating, interpreting, summarizing, and explaining cultural references, facilitate communication and understanding between speakers of different languages and cultural backgrounds (Coste et al., 2009). Mediation, as detailed in the CEFR 2020, involves several key aspects: mediating a text, mediating concepts, and mediating communication. Mediating a text includes activities such as relaying specific information, explaining data, and translating written texts. Mediating concepts involves activities like collaborating to construct meaning, leading group discussions, and managing collaborative interactions. Mediating communication focuses on facilitating communication in delicate situations, ensuring mutual understanding, and fostering a supportive communication environment (Council of Europe, 2020, pp. 90–121).

Unlike traditional language learning, which emphasizes the mastery of one or two languages in isolation, DIGICOMPASS seeks to develop a comprehensive linguistic repertoire. This approach aligns well with the CEFR's vision of language education, which emphasizes the integrated development of linguistic and cultural competencies. Language learning is a crucial component of the broader concept of language education. Within the DIGICOMPASS framework, this evolves into global language education. Global language education is defined as the process of developing linguistic and cultural competencies that prepare students to communicate and interact across multiple languages and cultural contexts. It is a necessary component of global citizenship, which involves understanding and respecting cultural diversity, fostering intercultural dialogue, and engaging responsibly in a globalized world (Deardorff, 2020; Inguaggiato, 2022; OECD, 2021, 2022; Risager, 2006).

DIGICOMPASS is an interdisciplinary modular framework that prioritizes language use. It encourages students to apply their language skills in real-world contexts, promoting active and meaningful communication. This approach aligns with the CEFR's action-oriented approach, viewing learners as social agents and language as a tool for accomplishing tasks and engaging in social interactions. Each module within the DIGICOMPASS framework specifies the CEFR proficiency levels required for various language activities, ensuring that students are prepared to perform tasks and interact in various linguistic contexts. The modules detail the lexical and grammatical competencies necessary for success, aligning language use with CEFR descriptors for proficiency standards.

While DIGICOMPASS emphasizes language use, it does not exclude traditional language learning activities. These activities remain an essential part of the curriculum. Students engage in structured learning experiences designed to develop their linguistic competence. These foundational skills are then applied in the DIGICOMPASS modules, where students use their language abilities to perform meaningful tasks and engage in intercultural communication. The CEFR's action-oriented approach significantly modifies the aim of language education. It no longer seeks mere mastery of individual languages but aims to develop a linguistic repertoire in which all linguistic abilities are interconnected.

This approach aligns with DIGICOMPASS's goals in several ways. First, the CEFR emphasizes that languages are not isolated but interconnected, and all linguistic experiences contribute to communicative competence. DIGICOMPASS similarly encourages learners to draw on their entire linguistic and cultural repertoire, using their knowledge of multiple languages to enhance communication and understanding. This perspective is supported by García and Wei (2014), who explore how translanguaging practices in education promote the use of multiple languages as integrated, dynamic systems rather than separate entities. Second, instead of aiming for balanced mastery of different languages, the CEFR focuses on the ability to modulate language use according to the social and communicative situation. DIGICOMPASS also prioritizes communicative flexibility, preparing students to adapt their language use to different cultural contexts and purposes. Byram et al. (2014) highlight the importance of developing intercultural competence alongside linguistic skills, enabling learners to understand and respect cultural differences and communicate effectively in diverse settings. Third, the CEFR acknowledges that barriers between languages can be overcome in communication, allowing for the purposeful use of different languages within the same interaction. DIGICOMPASS supports this view by promoting plurilingual and intercultural education, encouraging students to use multiple languages fluidly and strategically, as emphasized by CEFR 2020.

By integrating these elements, a DIGICOMPASS curriculum creates a dynamic and responsive learning environment. For instance, students might engage in projects that require them to research and present on various cultural practices, drawing on their linguistic and cultural backgrounds as well as those of the target culture. They might also participate in role-plays and simulations that require them to navigate and mediate between different cultural perspectives, developing both their linguistic skills and intercultural sensitivity. DIGICOMPASS focuses on developing a linguistic repertoire where all languages and cultural experiences are interrelated and interconnected. This approach aligns with the CEFR's vision of language education, which emphasizes the co-construction of meaning through interaction and views the learner as a social agent.

In sum, DIGICOMPASS integrates intercultural competence with plurilingualism, linguistic, sociolinguistic, and pragmatic competence, along with mediation strategies, to create a holistic and dynamic learning environment. This approach aligns with the broader goals of the CEFR, promoting intercultural dialogue, understanding, and cooperation in an increasingly interconnected global community.

2.4 Leveraging Adaptive Learning Technologies in Multiliteracies

Digital technologies play a pivotal role in enhancing multiliteracies by providing diverse tools and platforms that facilitate communication, collaboration, and creativity. Within DIGICOMPASS, adaptive learning technologies are crucial for making educational content accessible and engaging for all students. By personalizing learning experiences to match each student's proficiency level and learning pace, these technologies ensure that all learners can develop critical digital competencies, fostering an inclusive educational environment. These findings are further supported by Kim et al. (2021), who highlight how digital tools can enrich multiliteracies pedagogy, and Kalantzis and Cope (2023), who continue to refine the theoretical framework in response to evolving digital landscapes. Building on this foundation, DIGICOMPASS incorporates adaptive learning technologies to ensure all students have equal opportunities to succeed, aligning with broader educational goals of equity and inclusion as highlighted by Warschauer (2004), Lankshear and Knobel (2011), and Gottschalk and Weise (2023), who underscore the importance of digital equity and inclusion in education, particularly through the use of adaptive technologies in underserved communities.

The empirical effectiveness of adaptive learning technologies is well-documented in recent studies. Alrawashdeh et al. (2024) conducted a global meta-analysis, demonstrating that personalized and adaptive learning technologies significantly enhance reading literacy by tailoring educational experiences to individual learner needs. Similarly, Guo et al. (2023) found that blended learning approaches incorporating adaptive technologies markedly improve learners' self-efficacy and willingness to communicate, further supporting the case for these tools in personalized education. Jiang (2017) illustrates the potential of digital multimodal composing with adaptive technologies to boost language acquisition and engagement, particularly by allowing students to engage with content across multiple modes, thereby fostering a deeper understanding and retention of information. Xia et al. (2024) highlight the role of AI-driven adaptive learning systems in improving cross-cultural communication skills, emphasizing the importance of cultural sensitivity in language education. Additionally, Pennington et al. (2024) emphasize that targeted professional development for teachers enhances the effectiveness of adaptive learning technologies, leading to better student outcomes. Moreover, Wang et al. (2024) underscore the significant improvement in academic performance and learner motivation when adaptive learning systems are implemented, noting that these technologies also reduce the achievement gap among students from different socio-economic backgrounds.

The broader implications of these studies suggest that adaptive learning technologies have the potential to revolutionize education by creating more inclusive and equitable learning environments. These technologies not only cater to the diverse needs of learners but also promote engagement and self-efficacy, essential components of effective education. By addressing individual learning gaps and providing real-time feedback, adaptive learning systems contribute to a more personalized and responsive educational experience. This transformation is particularly critical in reducing educational disparities, ensuring that all students, regardless of their background, have access to high-quality learning opportunities that meet their specific needs. The integration of these technologies into educational practices could, therefore, play a key role in achieving broader educational equity and excellence.

To achieve its pedagogical aims, DIGICOMPASS draws on an extensive array of digital technologies. AI-driven adaptive learning technologies, which rely heavily on natural language processing (NLP), play a central role in creating personalized learning pathways and enhancing student engagement. NLP, as a core subfield of AI, enables machines to understand, interpret, and generate human language. This is crucial for developing systems that interact naturally with users. According to Jurafsky and Martin (2024), NLP algorithms such as text classification, sequence labeling, and neural network-based models underpin adaptive learning technologies. These technologies analyze learner input, provide instant feedback, and adjust educational materials to suit individual proficiency levels, thereby ensuring that educational content is finely tuned to each student's needs.

In the realm of language education, speech recognition and production technologies have become increasingly integral. Jurafsky and Martin (2024) highlight how advancements in Automatic Speech Recognition (ASR) and Text-to-Speech (TTS) systems are transforming the way learners engage with language. ASR technology allows learners to practice speaking and receive immediate feedback on pronunciation and fluency, while TTS systems provide examples of native pronunciation, aiding in the development of listening and speaking skills. These technologies are particularly effective in creating adaptive learning environments that adjust to the learner's progress, ensuring a customized and responsive educational experience.

Recent studies further underscore the transformative impact of NLP and AI-driven adaptive systems in education. Kökver et al. (2024) explore the use of NLP in detecting student misconceptions, demonstrating how AI applications can effectively analyze student responses in real-time, identifying misunderstandings, and providing immediate corrective feedback. This aligns with the concepts discussed by Jurafsky and Martin (2024) on the application of sequence labeling and dependency parsing techniques to enhance educational feedback mechanisms. Similarly, Lin et al. (2023) review the role of AI in intelligent tutoring systems, emphasizing their contribution to sustainable education by creating adaptive learning environments that respond to individual student needs. They highlight how foundational NLP methods, such as machine learning-based text analysis and neural language models, are instrumental in personalizing learning experiences, fostering long-term educational sustainability.

In a complementary direction, Vichare et al. (2024) present Qgen, an innovative system using NLP for question generation and answer evaluation. Their findings indicate that Qgen significantly enhances student engagement by generating contextually relevant questions and providing precise answer evaluations. This use of NLP techniques, including word sense disambiguation and part-of-speech tagging, supports the development of interactive assessments, echoing Jurafsky and Martin's (2024) discussions on the role of transformers and question-answering models in education. Finally, Qin and Zhong (2024) explore an AI-based adaptive system for English-speaking learning, revealing that such systems greatly improve language proficiency by adjusting exercise difficulty according to the learner's progress. Their research demonstrates the effectiveness of AI-driven adaptive systems in continuously monitoring learner performance and providing personalized feedback, which is crucial for developing speaking abilities—a concept reinforced by the NLP-driven adaptive learning technologies discussed by Jurafsky and Martin (2024).

Together, these studies highlight the potential of AI and NLP technologies in creating adaptive learning environments that not only meet individual learner needs but also enhance engagement and educational outcomes. By leveraging these technologies, educators can deliver more personalized and effective learning experiences, which are particularly valuable in today's diverse and dynamic educational landscape. The broader implications suggest that AI-driven adaptive systems will be central to the future of personalized education, playing a key role in improving learning outcomes across various domains.

Figure 2.2 provides a comprehensive visual representation of the data-driven processes involved in adaptive learning technologies, highlighting how various types of student data are collected, processed, and analyzed to personalize learning experiences within an educational framework. This flowchart illustrates the journey from initial data input, through processing, to the final output stage, where personalized learning paths, content customization, and real-time feedback converge to create an optimized learning environment.

At the Input Stage, cognitive, behavioral, and environmental data are collected to form the foundation of the adaptive learning process. These diverse data types are first funneled into the Processing Stage, where Data

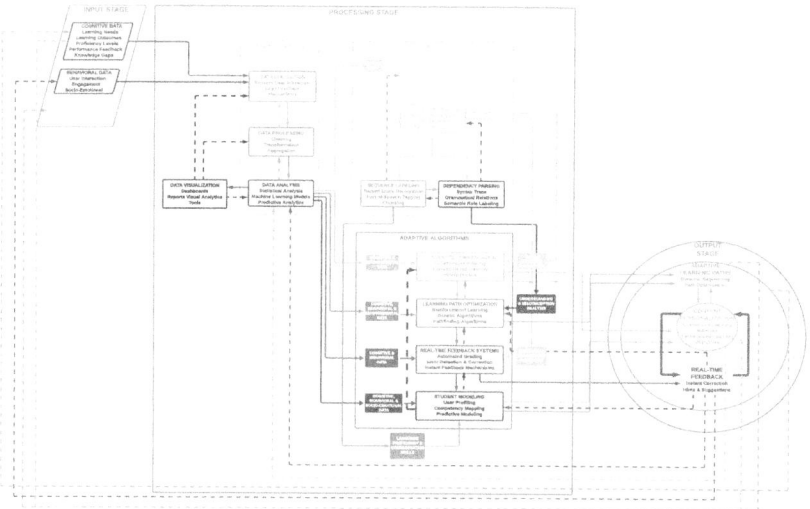

Fig. 2.2 Data-driven personalization in adaptive learning

Analytics plays a crucial role in cleaning, processing, and analyzing the data. Depending on the type of data, it may then be directed toward either NLP or Adaptive Algorithms. For instance, behavioral and socio-emotional data might influence the Student Modeling and Real-Time Feedback Systems within the Adaptive Algorithms box, ensuring that content personalization and adaptive learning paths are finely tuned to meet each student's needs. On the other hand, textual data might flow through the NLP module, where it undergoes processes such as tokenization and sentiment analysis to extract meaningful insights that further guide the adaptive learning algorithms. The Output Stage demonstrates how these processed inputs culminate in adaptive learning paths and personalized content delivery. The dashed lines in the chart represent feedback loops, where real-time feedback and content personalization can prompt a reevaluation of student data, leading to continuous adjustments in the learning environment.

Adaptive learning technologies, enhanced by AI and data analytics, are designed to continuously monitor student progress, analyze interactions, and adjust content and pacing accordingly. By collecting extensive data from student interactions—such as responses, time spent on tasks, and completion rates—these systems use advanced algorithms to identify trends, strengths, weaknesses, and learning preferences. This data-driven approach ensures that educational content is dynamically adjusted to match each student's needs, thereby optimizing the learning experience (Mejeh & Rehm, 2024). Platforms like DreamBox and Knewton exemplify how AI, NLP, and data analytics can work together to create dynamic learning environments where content is continuously adjusted to meet the evolving needs of students. These platforms incorporate adaptive learning systems that provide real-time feedback, ensuring that each student progresses at their own pace and achieves optimal learning outcomes.

While some adaptive learning technologies rely on pre-set rules and simpler algorithms, these systems do not adapt over time and lack the advanced data analysis capabilities of AI-driven solutions. Such rule-based systems are limited in their ability to provide personalized learning experiences that evolve with the learner's needs. In contrast, AI-driven adaptive learning technologies, such as those highlighted by Wang et al. (2024), are capable of continuously learning from student interactions, providing tailored feedback, and dynamically adjusting content in real-time to better meet individual learner needs. This approach has been shown to significantly improve learner outcomes, including engagement, motivation, and academic performance. Moreover, the integration of AI in education, as reviewed by Ayeni et al. (2024), emphasizes the superior capabilities of AI-driven adaptive systems in creating highly personalized and effective learning experiences. These systems leverage AI to analyze vast amounts of student data, enabling a level of personalization and adaptability that is not achievable with simpler, rule-based technologies. This makes AI-driven adaptive learning the primary focus in advanced educational settings like DIGICOMPASS, where the goal is to optimize learning outcomes through innovative, data-driven approaches.

The integration of AI adaptive learning technologies with other educational technologies creates a comprehensive and dynamic learning environment. Collaborative platforms such as Google Workspace and Microsoft Teams benefit from AI by providing insights into group dynamics and individual contributions, facilitating more effective collaboration (Nguyen et al., 2024). AI can monitor student participation in these collaborative settings, ensuring that all members are engaged and that group work is balanced. Similarly, AI-driven personalized learning paths within gamified environments, as discussed by Yekollu et al. (2024), ensure that challenges are tailored to each student's skill level, maintaining engagement and promoting continuous improvement.

Gamification platforms like Kahoot! and Classcraft use AI to create adaptive learning experiences that are both enjoyable and educational, adjusting the difficulty of tasks and providing personalized rewards to keep students motivated. In the realm of assistive technologies, AI significantly enhances tools such as screen readers and speech-to-text applications, making education more accessible for students with disabilities, as highlighted by Barua et al. (2022). Furthermore, content delivery technologies, including Learning Management Systems (LMS) like Canvas and Moodle, utilize AI to provide personalized learning materials and ensure that content is accessible across multiple devices and formats, aligning with the future-focused vision of Education 4.0 described by Castro et al. (2024).

In addition to enhancing accessibility and personalization, DIGICOMPASS fosters a mindful approach to digital citizenship, emphasizing online safety, and privacy, managing digital footprints, and preventing cyberbullying. This approach is informed by current pedagogical research, such as Tangül and Soykan's (2021) work, which highlights the importance of equipping both teachers and students with the skills to engage thoughtfully and safely online. Their research, along with the findings of Martin et al. (2022), underscores the need for critical evaluation of information, understanding the long-term impact of digital footprints, and promoting respectful interactions in digital environments. The 2024 Common Sense Digital Citizenship Curriculum Evaluation Report (Abades-Barclay & Banaji, 2024) further supports these findings by demonstrating the positive impact of structured digital citizenship programs on students' understanding of online safety, privacy, and ethical engagement.

DIGICOMPASS also draws on Ribble's (2015) nine elements of digital citizenship, including digital access, commerce, communication, literacy, etiquette, law, rights and responsibilities, health and wellness, and security. These elements form a comprehensive framework for fostering responsible digital engagement. Capuno et al. (2022) emphasize the significance of integrating digital citizenship into education, preparing students to engage ethically in the digital world. This comprehensive approach not only equips students with the skills needed for critical digital literacy but also addresses the psychological and social aspects of technology use, encouraging balanced screen time, managing digital stress, and fostering positive online relationships. By incorporating these aspects into its framework, DIGICOMPASS ensures that students are well-prepared to navigate the digital world responsibly and ethically, contributing to their overall development as responsible digital citizens (Livingstone & Helsper, 2010; UNICEF, 2021).

2.5 Advancing Global Citizenship and Social Responsibility

DIGICOMPASS is dedicated to fostering global citizenship and social responsibility, preparing students to become active, ethical participants in a diverse and interconnected world. Global citizenship involves understanding and respecting cultural diversity, engaging in intercultural dialogue, and contributing to global society with a sense of social justice and sustainability. This concept emphasizes active participation in a connected world and the ability to address global challenges collaboratively. Social responsibility, an integral part of global citizenship, entails recognizing the impact of one's actions on others and the environment. It involves taking proactive steps to contribute positively to society and advocating for equity and justice. The interconnected nature of global citizenship and social responsibility is central to the DIGICOMPASS framework, which integrates various strategies to promote these values. This includes projects and activities that encourage students to explore global issues, understand their complexities, and develop solutions that contribute to sustainable development.

One key pedagogical approach is project-based learning, as detailed in Chap. 6. In this approach, students tackle real-world problems, collaborate with peers from diverse backgrounds, and reflect on their experiences. Project-based learning fosters critical thinking, empathy, and a sense of agency, as students engage in projects that address pressing issues such as climate change, poverty, and human rights. Within DIGICOMPASS, service learning is conceived as project-based learning, where students connect classroom learning with meaningful community service. This approach allows students to address both local and global challenges hands-on, helping them understand the importance of social responsibility and the impact they can have on their communities and beyond. These service-learning projects often involve partnerships with local organizations, providing students with opportunities to engage directly with societal challenges and contribute positively. Reflective practices, such as journaling and group discussions, are also integral to the DIGICOMPASS framework, encouraging students to critically evaluate their actions and the societal implications of their decisions. Through this reflection, students develop a deeper understanding of their roles as global citizens and the importance of acting responsibly.

Recent studies underscore the importance of integrating global citizenship and social responsibility into education. OECD (2018) highlights the need for fostering global competencies, emphasizing the role of education in preparing students for an inclusive and sustainable world. Similarly, Rieckmann (2018) emphasizes the role of education in sustainable development, stressing the need to equip students with the capabilities to address global challenges. DIGICOMPASS weaves these insights into its design, encouraging students to harness their language abilities and digital literacies for advocacy, ethical engagement, and societal change.

Integrating social responsibility with language education and digital literacy enables students to leverage their skills for cross-cultural understanding and advocacy. Banks (2006) advocates for an educational model that promotes diversity and global citizenship, highlighting the importance of preparing students for a diverse world. DIGICOMPASS's adherence to the United Nations Sustainable Development Goals (SDGs), particularly SDG 4 (Quality Education), emphasizes its commitment to inclusive and equitable quality education and lifelong learning opportunities for all. The SDGs are designed to be a "blueprint to achieve a better and more sustainable future for all" (United Nations, 2015, p. 3) by addressing global challenges such as poverty, inequality, climate change, environmental degradation, peace, and justice. DIGICOMPASS's alignment with SDG 4 underscores its dedication to providing high-quality, accessible education that respects and integrates diverse cultural identities.

To promote social responsibility, DIGICOMPASS incorporates practical activities and resources, as suggested by Oxfam (2015), to teach students about global citizenship and ethical engagement. Oxfam describes global citizenship in education as encompassing awareness of global issues, a sense of connection to a worldwide community, and the empowerment to effect positive change. These activities include project-based learning and community engagement initiatives that help students understand and address global challenges, fostering a sense of social responsibility and global competence.

Incorporating the concept of mobility in a globalized world is pivotal to embracing a full spectrum of global citizenship within the DIGICOMPASS curriculum. Mobility encompasses the capability to navigate across various cultural and geographical landscapes, intellectual movements, and the evolving dynamics of globalized societies. It reflects the importance of understanding our place within the continuum of time, appreciating how historical events shape present conditions, and how present actions will impact future generations (Seixas, 1993; Urry, 2007). The framework seeks to cultivate this temporal perspective, enabling students to project the long-term consequences of today's decisions (Szerszynski & Urry, 2006).

The concept of mobility applies to global citizenship and DIGICOMPASS by encouraging students to think beyond immediate circumstances and consider the broader implications of their actions on a global scale. It emphasizes the interconnectedness of societies and the importance of fostering a global mindset that is aware of the impact of local actions on the global community. By encouraging students to understand and navigate the complexities of a globalized world, DIGICOMPASS helps them develop a more comprehensive and empathetic worldview. Rieckmann (2018) emphasizes the need for education systems to develop students' capabilities to contribute to sustainable development, reinforcing the importance of integrating social responsibility into the curriculum. Similarly, UNESCO (2020) outlines strategic approaches to embedding sustainability in education, aligning with DIGICOMPASS's objectives.

The DIGICOMPASS approach to social responsibility extends beyond immediate boundaries, instilling in students a profound understanding of the ethical implications of their actions on a global scale. It encompasses a dedication to making choices that contribute positively to the collective well-being of the global community, informed by an ethos of intergenerational equity and the desire to leave a sustainable legacy for future generations. Jonas (1984) underscores the importance of considering the long-term impacts of our actions and the moral responsibility we have to future generations, highlighting the need for educators to foster a sense of responsibility that transcends time and space. By promoting a culture of social responsibility, DIGICOMPASS empowers students to make informed, compassionate decisions that encourage philanthropy and service, which are fundamental to the spirit of global citizenship. Thus, social responsibility guides students as they navigate the complexities of a globalized world, ensuring their growth as agents of sustainable and positive change, shaping not only their present but also the world of tomorrow.

2.6 Conclusion

In revisiting the compass metaphor, the DIGICOMPASS framework emerges as the quintessential navigator through the intricate landscape of twenty-first-century global citizenship, transcending geographical and cultural boundaries and preparing students to thrive in a globally interconnected community.

The cardinal points of the compass—Digital Literacy, Inclusive Practices, Intercultural Competence, and Awareness of Social Strategies—each play a pivotal role in guiding learners through the multifaceted realm of contemporary education. Digital literacy, the North Star of our compass, illuminates the path toward mastering the digital domain, an essential skill in today's globalized world. Inclusive practices, shining from the East, ensure that this journey is accessible to students from all walks of life, championing equity and diversity in educational opportunities. To the South, intercultural competence encourages exploring and embracing the richness of the world's cultures, fostering mutual understanding and respect. Finally, from the West, awareness of social strategies prompts reflection on the societal impacts of our learning and actions, urging a commitment to ethical engagement and social responsibility.

By synthesizing these elements, DIGICOMPASS presents a holistic framework that integrates technological proficiency with cultural awareness and social consciousness, setting a new standard for language education in the digital age. This framework goes beyond language teaching to cultivate global citizens equipped to navigate, contribute to, and transform the world around them. Thus, as we conclude, it is evident that DIGICOMPASS represents the power of education to unite us across borders, fostering a future where people are not only fluent in multiple languages but also adept at navigating the complexities of our global society with empathy, understanding, and a drive to make a positive impact.

References

Abades-Barclay, F., & Banaji, S. (2024). *LSE - Common sense digital citizenship curriculum evaluation*. London School of Economics, Department of Media and Communications. https://www.lse.ac.uk/News/News-Assets/PDFs/2024/LSE-%E2%80%94-Common-Sense-Digital-Citizenship-Curriculum-Evaluation-Report-high-res-web-version-V6.pdf

Alrawashdeh, G. S., Fyffe, S., Azevedo, R. F. L., & Castillo, N. M. (2024). Exploring the impact of personalized and adaptive learning technologies on reading literacy: A global meta-analysis. *Educational Research Review, 42*, 100587.
AM, M. A., Hadi, S., Istiyono, E., & Retnawati, H. (2023). Does differentiated instruction affect learning outcome? Systematic review and meta-analysis. *Journal of Pedagogical Research, 7*(5), 18–33. https://doi.org/10.33902/JPR.202322021
Ayeni, O. O., Al Hamad, N. M., Chisom, O. N., Osawaru, B., & Adewusi, O. E. (2024). AI in education: A review of personalized learning and educational technology. *GSC Advanced Research and Reviews, 18*(2), 261–271.
Banks, J. A. (Ed.). (2006). *Diversity and citizenship education: Global perspectives.* Wiley.
Barua, P. D., Vicnesh, J., Gururajan, R., Oh, S. L., Palmer, E., Azizan, M. M., et al. (2022). Artificial intelligence enabled personalised assistive tools to enhance education of children with neurodevelopmental disorders – A review. *International Journal of Environmental Research and Public Health, 19*(3), 1192. https://doi.org/10.3390/ijerph19031192
Beacco, J. C., Byram, M., & Cavalli, M. (2016). *Guide for the development and implementation of curricula for plurilingual and intercultural education.* Council of Europe.
Bennett, M. J. (2013). *Basic concepts of intercultural communication: Paradigms, principles, and practices.* Intercultural Press.
Bornstein, D. (2007). *How to change the world: Social entrepreneurs and the power of new ideas.* Oxford University Press.
Byram, M. (2020). *Teaching and assessing intercultural communicative competence: Revisited.* Multilingual Matters.
Byram, M., Barrett, M., Lázár, I., Mompoint-Gaillard, P., & Philippou, S. (2014). *Developing intercultural competence through education.* Council of Europe Publishing.
Capuno, R., Suson, R., Suladay, D., Arnaiz, V., Villarin, I., & Jungoy, E. (2022). Digital citizenship in education and its implication. *World Journal on Educational Technology: Current Issues, 14*(2), 426–437. https://doi.org/10.18844/wjet.v14i2.6952
CAST. (2024). *Universal Design for Learning Guidelines version 3.0.* CAST. https://udlguidelines.cast.org
Castro, G., Chiappe, A., Rodriguez, D., & Sepulveda, F. (2024). Harnessing AI for education 4.0: Drivers of personalized learning. *Electronic Journal of e-Learning, 22*, 1–14. https://doi.org/10.34190/ejel.22.5.3467
Chan, B. S., Churchill, D., & Chiu, T. K. (2017). Digital literacy learning in higher education through digital storytelling approach. *Journal of International Education Research, 13*(1), 1–16.

Cipriano, C., & McCarthy, M. F. (2023). Towards an inclusive social and emotional learning. *Social and Emotional Learning: Research, Practice, and Policy, 2*, 100008.

Coste, D., Moore, D., & Zarate, G. (2009). *Plurilingual and pluricultural competence. Studies towards a common European framework of reference for language learning and teaching*. Council of Europe.

Council of Europe. (2001). *Common European framework of reference for languages: Learning, teaching, assessment*. Cambridge University Press. https://rm.coe.int/1680459f97

Council of Europe. (2020). *Common European framework of reference for languages: Learning, teaching, assessment – Companion volume*. Council of Europe. https://rm.coe.int/common-european-framework-of-reference-for-languages-learning-teaching/16809ea0d4

Coyle, D., Hood, P., & Marsh, D. (2010). *CLIL: Content and language integrated learning*. Cambridge University Press.

Deardorff, D. K. (2020). *Manual for developing intercultural competencies: Story circles*. UNESCO Publishing.

Deunk, M. I., Smale-Jacobse, A. E., de Boer, H., Doolaard, S., & Bosker, R. J. (2018). Effective differentiation practices: A systematic review and meta-analysis of studies on the cognitive effects of differentiation practices in primary education. *Educational Research Review, 24*, 31–54.

Eshet-Alkalai, Y. (2004). Digital literacy: A conceptual framework for survival skills in the digital era. *Journal of Educational Multimedia and Hypermedia, 13*(1), 93–106.

García, O., & Wei, L. (2014). *Translanguaging: Language, bilingualism and education*. Palgrave Macmillan.

Gay, G. (2018). *Culturally responsive teaching: Theory, research, and practice*. Teachers College Press.

Gee, J. P. (2015). *Social linguistics and literacies: Ideology in discourses*. Routledge.

Gibbs, K. (2022). Voices in practice: Challenges to implementing differentiated instruction by teachers and school leaders in an Australian mainstream secondary school. *The Australian Educational Researcher, 2023*(50), 1217–1232.

Gligorea, I., Cioca, M., Oancea, R., Gorski, A.-T., Gorski, H., & Tudorache, P. (2023). Adaptive learning using artificial intelligence in e-learning: A literature review. *Education Sciences, 13*(12), 1216.

Gottschalk, F., & Weise, C. (2023). Digital equity and inclusion in education: An overview of practice and policy in OECD countries. *OECD Education Working Papers*, No. 299.

Greenhow, C., Galvin, S., & Staudt Willet, K. B. (2019). What should be the role of social media in education? *Policy Insights from the Behavioral and Brain Sciences, 6*(2), 178–185.

Guo, Y., Wang, Y., & Ortega-Martín, J. (2023). The impact of blended learning-based scaffolding techniques on learners' self-efficacy and willingness to communicate. *Porta Linguarum, 40*(2), 253–273.

Harkins Monaco, E. A., Brusnahan, L. S., & Fuller, M. (2023). Guidance for the antiracist educator: Culturally sustaining pedagogies for disability and diversity. *Teaching Exceptional Children, 55*(5), 296–299.

Hattie, J. (2012). *Visible Learning for teachers: Maximizing impact on learning*. Routledge.

Inguaggiato, C. (Ed.). (2022). *Multilingual Global Education Digest 2022*. Università di Bologna. https://amsacta.unibo.it/id/eprint/7164/1/Koine_Multilingual_Global_Education%20Digest_2022.pdf

Jackson, J. (2019). *Introducing language and intercultural communication*. Routledge.

Jenkins, H., Ito, M., & boyd, D. (2016). *Participatory culture in a networked era: A conversation on youth, learning, commerce, and politics*. Polity Press.

Jiang, L. (2017). The affordances of digital multimodal composing for EFL learning. *ELT Journal, 71*(4), 413–422.

Jonas, H. (1984). *The imperative of responsibility: In search of an ethics for the technological age*. University of Chicago Press.

Jurafsky, D., & Martin, J. H. (2024). Speech and language processing: An introduction to natural language processing, computational linguistics, and speech recognition with language models (3rd ed.). Online manuscript released August 20, 2024. https://web.stanford.edu/~jurafsky/slp3

Kalantzis, M., & Cope, W. (2023). Multiliteracies: A short update. *The International Journal of Literacies, 30*(2), 1–15.

Kim, M. S., Meng, X., & Kim, M. (2021). Technology-enhanced multiliteracies teaching towards a culturally responsive curriculum: A multiliteracies approach to ECE. *Interactive Learning Environments, 31*(4), 1988–2000.

Kökver, Y., Pektaş, H. M., & Çelik, H. (2024). Artificial intelligence applications in education: Natural language processing in detecting misconceptions. *Educational Information Technology*, 1–32.

Kramsch, C. (1993). *Context and culture in language teaching*. Oxford University Press.

Lankshear, C., & Knobel, M. (2011). *New literacies: Everyday practices and social learning* (3rd ed.). McGraw-Hill Education.

Lin, C. C., Huang, A. Y. Q., & Lu, O. H. T. (2023). Artificial intelligence in intelligent tutoring systems toward sustainable education: A systematic review. *Smart Learning Environments, 10*, 41.

Livingstone, S., & Helsper, E. (2010). Balancing opportunities and risks in teenagers' use of the internet: The role of online skills and internet self-efficacy. *New Media & Society, 12*(2), 309–329.

Llinares, A., & Cross, R. (2022). New challenges for CLIL research: Identifying (in)equity issues. *AILA Review, 35*(2), 169–179.

Martin, F., Gezer, T., & Wang, C. (2022). Examining K-12 educator experiences from digital citizenship professional development. *Journal of Research on Technology in Education, 54*(1), 143–160. https://doi.org/10.1080/15391523.2020.1815611

Mejeh, M., & Rehm, M. (2024). Taking adaptive learning in educational settings to the next level: Leveraging natural language processing for improved personalization. *Educational Technology Research and Development, 72*, 1597–1621. https://doi.org/10.1007/s11423-024-10345-1

Nguyen, A., Kremantzis, M. D., Essien, A., Petrounias, I., & Hosseini, S. (2024). Enhancing student engagement through artificial intelligence (AI): Understanding the basics, opportunities, and challenges. *Journal of University Teaching and Learning Practice, 21*. https://doi.org/10.53761/caraaq92

OECD. (2018). *Preparing our youth for an inclusive and sustainable world: The OECD PISA global competence framework*. OECD Publishing.

OECD. (2021). *Global competency for an inclusive world*. OECD Publishing.

OECD. (2022). *Education for a changing world: How to ensure global competence for all*. OECD Publishing.

Oxfam. (2015). *Education for global citizenship: A guide for schools*. Oxfam GB.

Pennington, V., Howell, E., Kaminski, R., Ferguson-Sams, N., Gazioglu, M., Mittapalli, K., Banerjee, A., & Cole, M. (2024). Multilingual teaching and digital tools: The intersections of new media literacies and language learning. *Journal for Multicultural Education, 18*(1/2), 126–138. https://open.clemson.edu/cgi/viewcontent.cgi?article=1048&context=ed_human_dvlpmnt_pub

Qin, L., & Zhong, W. (2024). Adaptive system of English-speaking learning based on artificial intelligence. *Journal of Electrical Systems, 20*(6s), 267–275.

Reimers, F. M. (2020). *Educating students to improve the world*. Springer.

Ribble, M. (2015). *Digital citizenship in schools: Nine elements all students should know* (3rd ed.). International Society for Technology in Education.

Rieckmann, M. (2018). Key themes in education for sustainable development. In A. Leicht, J. Heiss, & W. J. Byun (Eds.), *Issues and trends in education for sustainable development* (Vol. 5, pp. 61–84). UNESCO Publishing. https://unesdoc.unesco.org/ark:/48223/pf0000261803?posInSet=2&queryId=42c5eb1f-e7f9-410d-8032-65045371505b

Risager, K. (2006). *Language and culture: Global flows and local complexity*. Multilingual Matters.

Rocca, S. (2024). Navigating a global future: Charting inclusive paths and digital multiliteracies with DIGICOMPASS. In *Proceedings of the 14th international conference the future of education* (pp. 185–188). Filodiritto Editore.

Schön, D. A. (2010). Educating the reflective practitioner: Toward a new design for teaching and learning in the professions. *Australian Journal of Adult Learning, 50*(2), 448–451.

Schwartz, H. N., Skoog-Hoffman, A., Polman, J., Kelly, O., Bañales, J., & Jagers, R. (2023). *Integrated learning, integrated lives: Highlighting opportunities for transformative SEL within academic instruction.* Social and Emotional Learning Innovations Series. https://files.eric.ed.gov/fulltext/ED641320.pdf

Seixas, P. (1993). Historical understanding among adolescents in a multicultural setting. *Curriculum Inquiry, 23*(3), 301–327.

Shulman, L. S. (2005). Pedagogies. *Liberal Education, 91*(2), 18–25.

Spitzberg, B. H., & Changnon, G. (2009). Conceptualizing intercultural competence. In D. K. Deardorff (Ed.), *The SAGE handbook of intercultural competence* (pp. 2–52). SAGE Publications.

Szerszynski, B., & Urry, J. (2006). Visuality, mobility and the cosmopolitan: Inhabiting the world from afar. *The British Journal of Sociology, 57*(1), 113–131.

Taguchi, N. (2011). Pragmatic development as a dynamic, complex process: General patterns and case histories. *The Modern Language Journal, 95*(4), 605–623.

Tangül, H., & Soykan, E. (2021). Comparison of students' and teachers' opinions toward digital citizenship education. *Frontiers in Psychology, 12*, 752059. https://doi.org/10.3389/fpsyg.2021.752059

Tinmaz, H., Lee, Y. T., Fanea-Ivanovici, M., & Baber, H. (2022). A systematic review on digital literacy. *Smart Learning Environments, 9*(1), 21.

Tomlinson, C. A., & Imbeau, M. B. (2023). *Leading and managing a differentiated classroom* (2nd ed.). ASCD.

UNESCO. (2018). *A global framework of reference on digital literacy skills for indicator 4.4.2.* UNESCO Institute for Statistics. https://uis.unesco.org/sites/default/files/documents/ip51-global-framework-reference-digital-literacy-skills-2018-en.pdf

UNESCO. (2020). *Education for sustainable development: A roadmap.* UNESCO. https://unesdoc.unesco.org/ark:/48223/pf0000374802

UNICEF. (2021). *The state of the world's children 2021: On my mind – Promoting, protecting and caring for children's mental health.* UNICEF. https://www.unicef.org/reports/state-worlds-children-2021

United Nations. (2015). *Sustainable development goals.* https://sdgs.un.org/goals

Urry, J. (2007). *Mobilities.* Polity Press.

Vichare, S., Gawade, A., & Mangrulkar, R. (2024). Qgen: A unique question generation and answer evaluation technique using natural language processing. *Journal of Engineering Education Transformations, 38*(1), 122–135. https://journaleet.in/articles/qgen-a-unique-question-generation-and-answer-evaluation-technique-using-natural-language-processing

Walkington, C., & Bernacki, M. L. (2020). Appraising research on personalized learning: Definitions, theoretical alignment, advancements, and future directions. *Journal of Research on Technology in Education, 52*(3), 235–252.

Wang, X., Huang, R. T., Sommer, M., Pei, B., Shidfar, P., Rehman, M. S., Ritzhaupt, A. D., & Martin, F. (2024). The efficacy of artificial intelligence-enabled adaptive learning systems from 2010 to 2022 on learner outcomes: A meta-analysis. *Journal of Educational Computing Research., 62,* 1568–1603. https://doi.org/10.1177/07356331241240459

Warschauer, M. (2004). *Technology and social inclusion: Rethinking the digital divide.* MIT Press.

Xia, Y., Shin, S.-Y., & Kim, J.-C. (2024). Cross-Cultural Intelligent Language Learning System (CILS): Leveraging AI to facilitate language learning strategies in cross-cultural communication. *Applied Sciences, 14,* 5651.

Yekollu, R. K., Bhimraj Ghuge, T., Sunil Biradar, S., Haldikar, S. V., & Farook Mohideen Abdul Kader, O. (2024). AI-driven personalized learning paths: Enhancing education through adaptive systems. In R. Asokan, D. P. Ruiz, & S. Piramuthu (Eds.), *Smart data intelligence. ICSMDI 2024. Algorithms for intelligent systems.* Springer. https://doi.org/10.1007/978-981-97-3191-6_38

Yoon, B. (2023). Research synthesis on culturally and linguistically responsive teaching for multilingual learners. *Education Sciences, 13*(6), 557.

Zhao, Y. (2018). *What works may hurt – Side effects in education.* Teachers College Press.

CHAPTER 3

Theoretical and Technological Foundations of DIGICOMPASS

Abstract This chapter examines the integration of educational theories and advanced technologies to create personalized, inclusive, and adaptive learning environments. Grounded in Constructivism, Vygotsky's Sociocultural Theory, Cognitive Load Theory, and Connectivism, the framework emphasizes active learning, social interaction, and digital connectivity. Key technologies, including adaptive learning, assistive tools, immersive platforms, and gamification, enhance engagement, accessibility, and collaboration. The chapter highlights adaptive systems that tailor educational content to individual needs, assistive technologies ensuring inclusivity, and immersive tools offering experiential learning. These innovations support plurilingualism, digital literacy, and global language education while promoting ethical engagement and sustainability. Through data analytics and real-time feedback, educators can make informed decisions to optimize learning outcomes. DIGICOMPASS demonstrates the transformative potential of harmonizing theory and technology in advancing global education.

Keywords Adaptive learning · Constructivism · Interactionist approach · Intersecting technologies · Technological compatibility

3.1 INTRODUCTION

In contemporary education, the recognition of student diversity in terms of readiness, interests, and learning profiles has prompted the adoption of personalized learning as a fundamental teaching strategy. Personalized learning aims to tailor teaching environments, content, and approaches to meet the varied needs of each learner. The integration of various technologies—particularly adaptive, assistive, immersive, collaborative, analytic, content delivery, and gamification technologies—has significantly enhanced the capacity for personalized learning. These technologies offer educators dynamic tools to effectively address individual learning paths. DIGICOMPASS seamlessly integrates these various technologies to create a holistic and adaptive learning environment, where each technology type plays a specific role in enhancing different aspects of the educational experience.

This chapter delves into the theoretical foundations supporting personalized learning and the DIGICOMPASS framework, provides an overview of the technologies involved, details the role of each technology, and discusses their integration for a holistic learning experience. By examining these elements, we aim to demonstrate how personalized learning strategies and advanced technologies can be harmonized to create a dynamic and inclusive educational environment. To begin, we will explore the theoretical foundations that underpin the DIGICOMPASS framework, providing context for how these theories guide the integration and application of educational technologies.

3.2 DIGICOMPASS THEORETICAL FOUNDATIONS

The DIGICOMPASS framework integrates key educational theories to create a holistic, personalized, and collaborative learning environment, that is, Constructivism, Vygotsky's Sociocultural Theory, Cognitive Load Theory (CLT), and Connectivism.

Constructivism emphasizes active, student-centered learning where learners construct their own understanding through experiences and reflection. This principle guides the adaptation of content, processes, and products to meet individual learners' needs within the DIGICOMPASS framework. Students engage actively with the material, collaborate with peers, and reflect on their learning experiences, ensuring that learning is meaningful and deeply rooted in personal experiences (Piaget, 1970; Bruner, 1960; Dewey, 1938).

Vygotsky's Sociocultural Theory complements constructivism by emphasizing the importance of social interaction and cultural context in learning. The concept of scaffolding, where teachers provide support based on the learner's current level and gradually remove it as they become more proficient, is central to this theory. In DIGICOMPASS, scaffolding supports students' learning journeys, enabling them to progress at their own pace while engaging in meaningful social interactions (Vygotsky, 1978).

Cognitive Load Theory (CLT) focuses on managing the capacity of working memory to prevent overwhelming it. Effective personalization in DIGICOMPASS considers cognitive load by structuring information to align with learners' cognitive abilities. Lessons and activities are designed to be appropriately challenging without causing cognitive overload, ensuring efficient information processing and retention (Sweller, 1988).

Connectivism highlights the role of technology and networks in learning, asserting that knowledge is distributed across a network of connections. Learning involves the ability to construct and traverse these networks. In DIGICOMPASS, connectivism is reflected through the integration of digital tools and resources, fostering digital literacy and enabling students to build and navigate their own learning networks (Siemens, 2005).

Figure 3.1 illustrates how these theories intersect within the DIGICOMPASS framework to create a cohesive learning environment. Constructivism and Sociocultural Theory promote collaborative learning and scaffolding, while Constructivism and CLT ensure that learning activities are engaging and manageable. The overlap of Constructivism and Connectivism integrates technology into active learning and combining Sociocultural Theory and Connectivism enhances social learning through digital connectivity. Cognitive Load Theory and Connectivism work together to manage cognitive load in digital environments, whereas Sociocultural Theory and Connectivism intersect in virtual exchanges and online collaborative projects where students interact with peers from different cultural backgrounds. Similarly, integrating CLT and Connectivism ensures students can navigate digital networks without cognitive overload, using adaptive technologies that adjust content difficulty based on real-time assessments. With this theoretical grounding, we now turn to the diverse technologies in the DIGICOMPASS framework, each enhancing personalized learning.

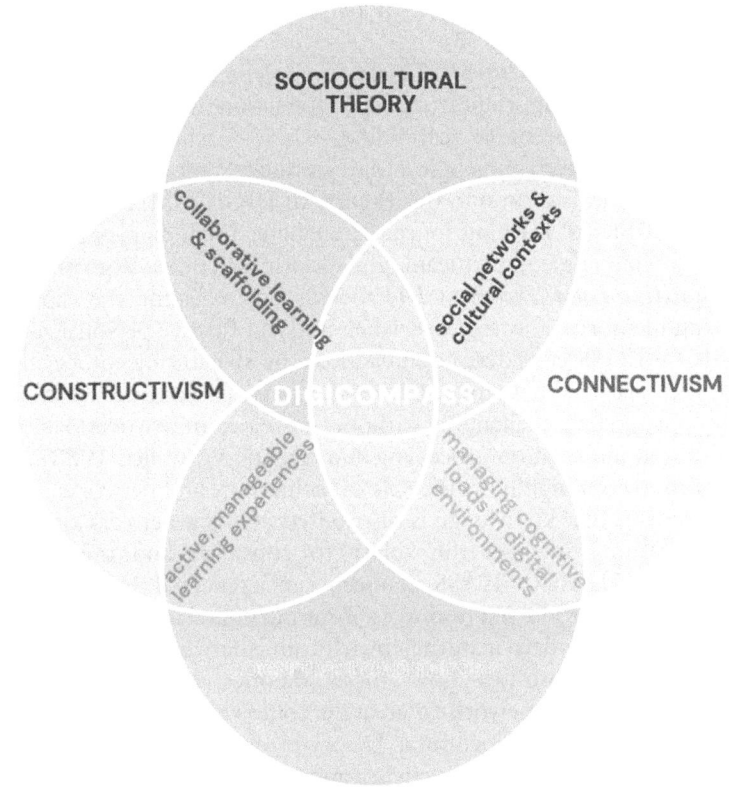

Fig. 3.1 DIGICOMPASS theoretical foundations

3.3 Overview of Technologies in DIGICOMPASS

DIGICOMPASS leverages a variety of technologies to create an inclusive, adaptive, and engaging learning environment that supports personalized and collaborative learning. These technologies not only tailor educational experiences to individual student needs but also foster effective communication and teamwork among learners and educators.

Adaptive learning technologies (Table 3.1) use algorithms and AI to customize educational content, adjusting the difficulty, pace, and style based on real-time data. This personalization aligns with Constructivism by providing interactive and engaging content that evolves based on

Table 3.1 Adaptive learning technologies in DIGICOMPASS

Description	Benefits	Examples
Data collection: Gathers information on answers, time spent, and success rates from student interactions with digital tools	Provides a comprehensive dataset to analyze student performance and tailor content accurately	Platforms like Khan Academy or Moodle (track user interaction and performance metrics), NotebookLM, (analyzes and summarizes user-provided documents)
Analysis and adjustment: Uses machine learning to evaluate learning pace, knowledge level, and gaps; adjusts content difficulty	Ensures content is optimally challenging for each student, enhancing learning efficiency	Adaptive algorithms in platforms like DreamBox or Knewton (adjust tasks based on real-time data), Brisk Teaching (tailors lesson plans dynamically)
Personalized learning paths: Customizes problems and topics based on individual performance, providing targeted revision and advanced material	Promotes mastery by addressing specific educational needs, improving academic outcomes	Smart Sparrow, adaptive learning modules in Coursera, Edmodo, Magic School AI, Diffit for Teachers (generates differentiated resources)
Adaptable learning paths: Automatically adjusts educational content in real-time to match the student's mastery of the material	Maximizes learning efficiency by keeping content challenging yet accessible at all times	Adaptive learning environments in platforms like Alek, Babbel, or ReadTheory adjusting text difficulty based on performance
Feedback loops: Offers real-time feedback to help students understand mistakes and correct them	Reinforces learning, boosts confidence, and fosters independent problem-solving skills	Immediate feedback systems in Duolingo or Quizlet Live that show correct answers and explanations, or Flint, which provides detailed, actionable feedback
User capability enhancement: Trains students and educators on effectively utilizing and understanding adaptive platforms	Empowers users to fully leverage technology, enhancing the educational experience	Workshops and online tutorials on using and maximizing EdTech tools like Smartboards or Google Classroom
Educational alignment: Ensures adaptive technologies support DIGICOMPASS's goals for academic and intercultural competence	Supports broad educational objectives, preparing students for global citizenship	Integration of adaptive tech in language learning programs like Mango Languages for intercultural competence

student responses, allowing learners to construct their own understanding through active participation.

Assistive technologies (Table 3.2) make digital content accessible to students with disabilities, promoting inclusivity and ensuring that all learners can participate effectively. This is consistent with Vygotsky's Sociocultural Theory, which emphasizes the importance of providing support (scaffolding) to learners at their current level of understanding.

Immersive technologies (Table 3.3) provide interactive and experiential learning environments, helping students to understand complex concepts more deeply. These technologies support Cognitive Load Theory by managing cognitive load through immersive experiences that present information in engaging and digestible formats.

Collaborative technologies (Table 3.4) facilitate communication and teamwork, enabling students and teachers to work together seamlessly, share resources, and engage in group projects. This reflects the principles of Vygotsky's Sociocultural Theory, which highlights the importance of social interactions and cultural context in learning. It also supports Connectivism by enabling learners to build and traverse networks of knowledge dynamically.

Table 3.2 Assistive technologies in DIGICOMPASS

Description	Benefits	Examples
Visual learning aids: Includes adaptive visual aids like graphs, videos, and animations that cater to varying mastery levels	Aids comprehension and retention, particularly for visual learners	Use of interactive simulations and videos in platforms like Edpuzzle or GeoGebra, ThingLink (interactive visuals), Wordwall (customizable visual activities)
Screen readers: Converts text to speech, enabling visually impaired students to access written content	Enhances accessibility for students with visual impairments	NVDA (NonVisual Desktop Access), ChromeVox
Speech-to-text tools: converts spoken words into text to assist students with writing difficulties	Supports students in completing assignments and participating in discussions	Google Docs Voice Typing, Microsoft Dictate
Alternative input devices: Devices such as adaptive keyboards or eye-tracking systems for students with physical disabilities	Enables all students to interact with digital content regardless of physical limitations	Adaptive keyboards, Tobii Eye Tracker

Table 3.3 Immersive technologies in DIGICOMPASS

Description	Benefits	Examples
Extended reality (XR): Encompasses VR, AR, and MR, creating immersive digital environments and experiences	Provides engaging and interactive learning experiences	Google Expeditions (AR/VR) for virtual field trips, CoSpaces Edu for creating and exploring 3D environments
Virtual reality (VR): Creates fully immersive computer-generated environments for experiential learning	Enhances engagement and understanding of complex concepts through simulations	Google Cardboard for affordable VR experiences, YouTube VR for 360-degree videos and simulations
Augmented reality (AR): Overlays digital information onto the real-world using devices like smartphones or AR glasses	Provides interactive and contextual learning experiences	QuiverVision for interactive AR coloring, Merge Cube for handheld AR activities, Thinglink for overlaying interactive media
Mixed reality (MR): Combines elements of VR and AR, allowing interaction between real and virtual objects	Facilitates interactive and immersive learning experiences	CoSpaces Edu for creating mixed-reality projects, Microsoft HoloLens for hands-on MR experiences, Thinglink for integrating virtual elements

Table 3.4 Collaborative technologies in DIGICOMPASS

Description	Benefits	Examples
Online collaboration platforms: Enable real-time document sharing, video conferencing, and instant messaging	Facilitates teamwork, resource sharing, and effective communication	Google Workspace (Google Docs, Sheets, Meet), Microsoft Teams (free educational licenses), Flint (creates collaborative assignments)
Interactive whiteboards: Allow multiple users to write or draw simultaneously, supporting interactive lessons and group activities	Enhances student engagement and collaborative learning	Jamboard (part of Google Workspace), Microsoft Whiteboard, Thinglink (adds collaborative interactive media elements)
Digital discussion forums: Provide platforms for students to engage in discussions and share resources	Encourages peer-to-peer interaction and collaborative problem-solving	Edmodo, Moodle forums, Khanmigo Teacher Tools (guides discussions and supports collaborative problem-solving)

Table 3.5 Data analytic technologies in DIGICOMPASS

Description	Benefits	Examples
Learning analytics dashboards: Aggregate data from various sources to provide insights into student performance and learning patterns	Helps educators make data-driven decisions to personalize instruction	Google Classroom (tracks student engagement and progress), Microsoft Education Insights (provides detailed performance reports), NotebookLM (analyzes and summarizes data for actionable insights)
Formative assessment tools: Provide immediate and constructive feedback on student performance	Guides students in their learning journey, promoting continuous improvement	Kahoot! (offers gamified quizzes with instant feedback), Socrative (delivers real-time results for formative assessments), Flint (customizes assessments and provides real-time feedback), Brisk Teaching (adjusts lessons dynamically based on student performance)
Performance dashboards: Track and display student progress and outcomes	Identify areas needing additional support and intervention	ClassDojo (visualizes individual and class-wide progress), Edmodo (tracks assignment submissions and engagement), Magic School AI (tracks progress and highlights areas for intervention), Wordwall (tracks performance metrics for interactive activities)

Data analytic technologies (Table 3.5) offer real-time insights into student performance, allowing educators to personalize instruction further and provide timely feedback. These tools help manage cognitive load by providing information that aligns with the learner's cognitive abilities and needs, in line with Cognitive Load Theory.

Content delivery technologies (Table 3.6) ensure that learning materials are accessible across various devices, supporting flexible, anytime, anywhere learning. This flexibility aligns with Connectivism, emphasizing the role of technology and networks in learning by providing access to diverse information sources and facilitating the construction of knowledge networks.

Gamification technologies (Table 3.7) enhance engagement and motivation by integrating game elements into educational activities, making learning more enjoyable. By providing interactive and motivating

Table 3.6 Content delivery technologies in DIGICOMPASS

Description	Benefits	Examples
E-learning platforms: Host course materials, interactive modules, and multimedia resources	Provides comprehensive and centralized access to educational content	Khan Academy (provides free lessons and practice activities), Coursera (offers structured online courses), Moodle (manages course materials and discussions), Magic School AI (generates interactive educational modules)
Mobile learning apps: Ensure that learning materials are accessible on smartphones and tablets	Supports flexible, anytime, anywhere learning	Duolingo (teaches languages with gamified lessons), Quizlet (offers flashcards and learning games), Khan Academy (provides mobile access to video lessons), Wordwall (offers interactive games accessible on mobile devices)
Multimedia content: Includes videos, podcasts, and interactive learning modules	Enhances engagement and caters to different learning styles	YouTube Education (hosts educational videos), TED-Ed (provides engaging video-based lessons), Thinglink (creates interactive multimedia resources), Textivate (generates interactive language practice content)

Table 3.7 Gamification technologies in DIGICOMPASS

Description	Benefits	Examples
Educational games: Incorporate game elements into learning activities to make them more engaging	Increases motivation and sustains student interest	Kahoot! (offers gamified quizzes), Quizizz (gamified learning platform), Wordwall (creates interactive, game-based learning activities)
Badges and leaderboards: Provide rewards and recognition for achievements and participation	Encourages competition and collaboration among students.	Classcraft (uses badges and leaderboards to encourage competition), Edmodo badges (recognizes achievements), Magic School AI (automatically creates badges for progress milestones)
Reward systems: Offer points, badges, and other incentives to motivate students	Makes learning more enjoyable and interactive	ClassDojo (tracks behavior and awards points), Habitica (turns tasks into a gamified experience)

experiences, these technologies support Constructivism and Sociocultural Theory by encouraging active participation and social interaction.

Together, these technologies form a comprehensive structure within the DIGICOMPASS framework, fostering a learning environment that is both personalized and collaborative, as well as theoretically grounded. Next, we will examine the specific roles and applications of these technologies within the DIGICOMPASS framework, illustrating how they contribute to a personalized and adaptive learning environment.

Adaptive learning technologies use algorithms and AI to tailor educational content to the individual learner's needs, adjusting the difficulty, pace, and content style based on real-time data. These systems start with a baseline assessment to gauge a student's knowledge and create a customized learning path that dynamically adjusts as the student progresses. By collecting data on student interactions, adaptive learning technologies analyze patterns, strengths, weaknesses, and learning preferences, allowing for real-time content adjustments. In a DIGICOMPASS curriculum, adaptive learning provides customized learning paths for each student, uses data analytics to monitor progress, and ensures that students receive appropriate challenges and support based on their learning needs. Complementing adaptive learning, assistive technologies play a critical role in ensuring accessibility and inclusivity, making educational content accessible to all students regardless of their disabilities.

Assistive technologies enhance accessibility for students with disabilities, ensuring they can access and participate effectively in the curriculum. Tools such as screen readers, speech-to-text software, and alternative input devices convert text to speech, spoken words to text, and physical movements into digital commands. In DIGICOMPASS, these technologies ensure that all digital content is accessible to students with visual, auditory, or motor impairments. They provide personalized support tools to meet individual needs and integrate universally designed learning principles to make the curriculum inclusive. Moving from accessibility to engagement, immersive technologies offer interactive and experiential learning opportunities that can transform the educational experience.

Immersive technologies, including VR, AR, and MR, create interactive and experiential learning environments. VR headsets immerse students in fully computer-generated environments, AR overlays digital information onto the physical world using devices like smartphones, and MR combines elements of both to allow interaction between real and virtual objects. In DIGICOMPASS, these technologies enable experiential learning through virtual field trips and simulations, enhance understanding of complex concepts through immersive visualizations, and facilitate cultural immersion experiences to foster intercultural competence. Equally important to the learning process are collaborative technologies, which facilitate communication and teamwork among students and educators, promoting a socially rich learning environment.

Collaborative technologies facilitate teamwork and communication among students through online platforms. Tools like Google Workspace and Microsoft Teams support real-time collaboration by enabling document sharing, video conferencing, and instant messaging. Interactive whiteboards allow multiple users to write or draw simultaneously. In DIGICOMPASS, these tools support group projects and collaborative learning activities, encourage peer-to-peer interaction and teamwork, and connect students with global communities for cultural exchange and collaborative problem-solving. To further enhance the learning experience, data analytic technologies provide valuable insights into student performance and learning patterns, enabling data-driven decisions that personalize instruction.

Data analytic technologies provide insights into student performance and learning patterns through data collection and analysis. Learning analytics dashboards aggregate data from LMS interactions, assignment submissions, and assessment results. Advanced algorithms analyze this data to identify trends, predict outcomes, and highlight areas needing intervention. Feedback technologies offer immediate and constructive feedback to students. In DIGICOMPASS, these tools track student progress, identify areas needing improvement, provide actionable insights for teachers, and offer immediate feedback to guide students' learning processes. In addition to analytics, content delivery technologies ensure that learning materials are accessible across various devices, supporting flexible, anytime-anywhere learning.

Content delivery technologies centralize and distribute educational content through e-learning platforms and mobile learning apps. These platforms host course materials, interactive modules, and multimedia resources, providing a comprehensive learning environment accessible on multiple devices, including smartphones, tablets, and computers. In DIGICOMPASS, content delivery technologies ensure that learning materials are accessible anywhere and anytime, use multimedia to cater to different learning needs, and provide on-demand access to educational resources. To make learning more engaging and enjoyable, gamification technologies integrate game elements into educational activities, increasing motivation and student interest.

Gamification technologies integrate game elements into educational activities to enhance engagement and motivation. These technologies use digital badges, points, leaderboards, and rewards to motivate students. Gamification software tracks student progress and achievements, offering real-time feedback and rewards for completing tasks. In DIGICOMPASS, gamification makes learning fun and engaging through interactive games, uses rewards and recognition to motivate students, and encourages competition and collaboration among students.

Finally, while each of these technologies offers unique benefits, their combined impact on language learning and plurilingualism is particularly profound. The following section explores these impacts in detail, highlighting how these technologies work together to enhance language education.

3.4 Impact of Technologies on Language Learning and Plurilingualism

This section explores how adaptive, immersive, collaborative, and assistive technologies enhance language learning and plurilingualism, linking them to the theoretical foundations discussed earlier in this chapter. Plurilingualism emphasizes the ability to use multiple languages flexibly across different contexts, a concept that resonates with the interactionist approach, which highlights the essential role of social interaction and communication in second language acquisition (SLA).

The interactionist approach (Mackey et al., 2013) is central to understanding SLA as it emphasizes the crucial role of social interaction and communication in learning a new language. This approach integrates the Input Hypothesis, which posits that language acquisition occurs through exposure to comprehensible input (Krashen, 1985), the Interaction Hypothesis, which highlights the importance of meaningful interaction and negotiation of meaning (Long, 1996), and the Output Hypothesis, which underscores the necessity of producing language for effective learning (Swain, 1985).

This centrality is further supported by its alignment with Vygotsky's Sociocultural Theory, which underscores the significance of social interaction and cultural context in cognitive development. Both paradigms see interaction as a mediator of learning, where learners co-construct knowledge through guided support and collaboration (Lantolf, 2000). Additionally, the ecological approach to language learning emphasizes the interconnectedness of learners with their social and symbolic environments, supporting the interactionist approach's focus on meaningful, contextualized interactions (van Lier, 2004). This aligns directly with Vygotsky's emphasis on the social nature of learning and the importance of cultural context.

Usage-based theories propose that language learning emerges from the dynamic interactions between cognitive processes and environmental input, resonating with the interactionist approach's emphasis on the importance of interaction. These theories highlight that linguistic knowledge is constructed from actual language use, emphasizing the role of frequency and context in learning. This perspective aligns with the interactionist approach as frequent, meaningful interactions help learners build and refine their language competence through exposure to varied and contextually rich language use. These theories support the constructivist underpinnings of the DIGICOMPASS framework, where learners actively construct their knowledge through experience and interaction (Ellis & Wulff, 2014).

Embodied cognition posits that cognitive processes are deeply rooted in bodily interactions with the world. This theory complements the interactionist approach by stressing that physical actions and sensory experiences during interactions enhance language comprehension and retention (Barsalou, 2008). Similarly, multimodality integrates various modes of communication (e.g., visual, auditory, and gestural) to provide a richer context for language learning. This aligns with the interactionist approach by emphasizing that multimodal input during interactions facilitates deeper understanding and retention of language. These theories also align with CLT within the DIGICOMPASS framework by using different ways of presenting information (such as visual, auditory, and textual inputs) to prevent overwhelming students and improve learning efficiency (Jewitt et al., 2016).

The concept of translanguaging also plays a significant role, as it reflects the use of all linguistic resources available to a learner. Translanguaging practices align with Vygotsky's Sociocultural Theory by emphasizing the role of social context and interaction in language use, enabling learners to navigate multiple languages fluidly (García & Wei, 2014). Collaborative technologies further facilitate translanguaging by supporting multilingual communication and cultural exchanges.

Technological advancements have significantly impacted these theoretical approaches and their application to language learning and plurilingualism. For example, AI-powered language learning apps such as Duolingo and Babbel provide personalized input tailored to the learner's proficiency level, delivering content that is both challenging and comprehensible (González-Lloret & Rock, 2022). These technologies ensure constant exposure to language input. Immersive technologies like VR and AR create lifelike environments for meaningful interactions, facilitating real-time communication with native speakers or peers, providing opportunities for negotiation of meaning. These tools promote language learning by providing immersive learning experiences, enhancing motivation, creating interaction, and reducing learning anxiety (Huang et al., 2021).

Additionally, digital technologies facilitate translanguaging practices by enabling students to engage in multilingual communication and cultural exchanges, aligning with sociocultural and ecological approaches (Wei, 2018). AI technologies have revolutionized language learning through personalized, adaptive, and interactive applications. Tools like Duolingo, Babbel, and Rosetta Stone use AI to provide personalized experiences, adapting to proficiency levels and offering real-time feedback. Studies have shown that personalized feedback significantly enhances language acquisition and retention (Lee & Lee, 2024; Han & Sari, 2024). However, overreliance on AI tools may lack cultural and pragmatic language use, which human teachers provide (Sung & Kang, 2024; Jeon, 2024). Barrot (2024) found that ChatGPT can develop receptive linguistic knowledge and oral communicative ability. Similarly, Loewen et al. (2020) demonstrated that app-based instruction effectively develops receptive linguistic knowledge and oral communicative ability. AI integration enables personalized learning pathways by adapting content and pacing to individual needs, with NLP providing tailored feedback and suggestions (Huang et al., 2023; Wei, 2023). AI-powered apps enhance the interactionist approach to SLA by providing meaningful input, facilitating interaction, and encouraging output through interactive exercises and immediate feedback (Akhiat, 2024).

Intelligent tutoring systems, such as Rosetta Stone and advanced features in Duolingo, use AI to analyze student performance and adapt instructional content. They offer targeted practice and feedback, helping learners overcome specific challenges in language learning. The adaptive nature of these systems ensures that learners remain engaged and progress at an optimal pace. Han and Sari (2024) highlight the effectiveness of intelligent tutoring systems, noting that they often outperform traditional methods in helping students grasp complex subjects. Like AI-powered language learning apps, intelligent tutoring systems enable personalized learning pathways by using NLP to analyze learner input and adjust the instructional content accordingly. This ensures that each learner receives a tailored educational experience that meets their specific needs and pace of learning (Lee & Lee, 2024). Intelligent tutoring systems facilitate interactive exercises that mimic real-life conversations, providing learners with immediate feedback and opportunities to modify their output. This interaction is critical for language development as it allows learners to test hypotheses and refine their language use (Jeon, 2024).

XR technologies, including VR and AR, create immersive environments where learners can practice language skills in lifelike contexts. For example, VR platforms like MondlyAR, Google Earth VR, and Labster can simulate real-world scenarios such as shopping in a foreign market or navigating a new city, enhancing language comprehension and cultural competence. Research has shown that immersive VR experiences can increase engagement and improve language retention (Familoni & Onyebuchi, 2024). Tafazoli (2024) highlights the role of extended reality in computer-assisted language learning, noting that these technologies enable personalized and interactive learning experiences. Schorr et al. (2024) found that augmented reality environments significantly enhance language learning by providing immersive and context-rich experiences.

Additionally, VR platforms create social environments where learners can interact with peers and native speakers in real-time, practicing language skills in meaningful contexts. This interaction supports language development by providing opportunities for negotiation of meaning and conversational adjustments (Tafazoli, 2024). MR platforms, such as Microsoft HoloLens, enable students to interact with both digital and physical objects, facilitating collaborative projects in a shared virtual space. This can be particularly beneficial for language learners working on group projects, where they can practice language skills in a collaborative setting (Familoni & Onyebuchi, 2024).

AI and data analytics significantly enhance plurilingualism and multilingualism by providing advanced tools for language learning and policy development. AI-driven content curation highlights contributions from various cultures and languages, promoting awareness and appreciation of plurilingual and multicultural contexts. This ensures learners are exposed to a wide array of linguistic resources, fostering a deeper understanding of different languages and cultures. Recent advancements show how AI can integrate diverse linguistic resources, making them more accessible and enhancing language learning processes (Bui & Namaziandost, 2023; Eren, 2024).

XR technologies also support plurilingualism and multilingualism through VR and AR applications. VR platforms like Google Expeditions allow learners to virtually visit different parts of the world, experiencing diverse cultures and languages. This immersive experience fosters intercultural competence and plurilingualism by exposing learners to various linguistic and cultural settings. Conrad et al. (2024) indicated that VR-based learning environments can significantly enhance language learning by providing immersive and interactive experiences. AR applications overlay digital content onto the physical world, providing contextual language learning experiences. For example, AR can be used in language classrooms to create interactive storytelling sessions, where students can explore cultural narratives in multiple languages. Bacca et al. (2014) noted a decade ago that AR trends in education significantly enhance engagement and contextual learning, making abstract concepts more tangible and relatable.

While the integration of AI and XR technologies offers numerous benefits, there are also critical considerations to address. Access to advanced technologies is often limited by socioeconomic factors, making it essential to ensure equitable access to AI and XR tools for inclusive language education. Developing low-cost or open-source versions of these technologies can help bridge the digital divide. Christanti et al. (2024) discuss the importance of addressing technological inequalities to ensure that all students have access to high-quality educational resources. AI algorithms may lack cultural sensitivity and fail to capture the nuances of language use in different cultural contexts.

Involving language and cultural experts in the development of AI and XR content can enhance cultural relevance and sensitivity. Kramsch (2014) emphasizes the need for cultural awareness in language teaching, which remains crucial as AI and XR technologies become more integrated into education. Overreliance on technology may undermine the role of human teachers, who provide essential cultural and pragmatic language instruction. Blended learning approaches that combine technology with human instruction can offer a balanced and comprehensive language learning experience. Recent research highlights the effectiveness of blended learning in integrating the strengths of both technological and human elements in education (European Commission, 2023; Zhang & Huang, 2024; Rezkilaturahmi et al., 2024).

In summary, the interactionist approach serves as a central framework in SLA, emphasizing the importance of social engagement and contextualized interactions in learning a new language. This aligns well with the theoretical underpinnings of the DIGICOMPASS framework, which leverages technologies such as AI-powered language learning apps, intelligent tutoring systems, and immersive XR (VR and AR) tools to support active engagement, social interaction, cognitive load management, and networked learning. Reflecting on the past two decades, Wang (2024) provides a comprehensive review of advancements in mobile-assisted language learning (MALL), highlighting significant technological developments like AI integration, adaptive learning systems, and VR for immersive experiences. Wang discusses the positive impact of these technologies on language acquisition, including improvements in learner engagement, interaction, and retention, while also addressing persistent challenges such as technological inequalities and the need for culturally sensitive AI algorithms. This retrospective underscores the importance of continued innovation and research in optimizing the benefits of technology for language learning and plurilingualism, leading to an exploration of how adaptive learning plays a central role in creating a dynamic and responsive educational environment in the next section.

3.5 Adaptive Learning as a Core Component of Holistic Learning

The DIGICOMPASS curriculum integrates various technologies to create a holistic and adaptive learning environment. Adaptive learning technologies are foundational because they dynamically adjust to individual student needs and interact with other technologies to enhance personalized learning. Importantly, personalized learning does not preclude collaboration; instead, it often incorporates collaborative tools and activities, fostering a socially rich learning environment.

Adaptive learning systems are central to personalized learning, adjusting to individual student needs and providing customized learning paths. Constructivism emphasizes active, student-centered learning, which adaptive systems support by offering interactive content that evolves based on student responses. Vygotsky's Sociocultural Theory underscores the importance of social interactions, and adaptive systems foster this through collaborative tools. Cognitive Load Theory (CLT) aims to optimize working memory capacity, with adaptive technologies customizing content complexity to enhance efficiency. Connectivism highlights technology's role in learning, supported by adaptive systems that integrate diverse information sources and digital tools.

To further understand the benefits and practical application of adaptive learning, we will explore evidence-based benefits and implementation strategies. The following section provides detailed insights into the effectiveness of adaptive learning technologies.

3.5.1 Adaptive Learning Technologies: Benefits and Implementation

Adaptive learning technologies are essential in contemporary education, especially within the DIGICOMPASS framework. These technologies utilize AI and advanced algorithms to tailor content to the unique needs of each student by analyzing their interactions with digital materials in real-time. This ensures a personalized learning experience that adjusts difficulty, pace, and preferences to keep students engaged and challenged. Adaptive technologies customize educational content, making learning more effective by catering to each student's abilities and needs. These systems analyze learners' responses and automatically adjust the difficulty of tasks, the pace of instruction, and the nature of support provided, aligning with each student's unique learning curve. This dynamic adjustment ensures appropriate difficulty for all students, enhancing engagement by maintaining appropriate levels of challenge and support.

Data-driven insights from adaptive systems enable educators to tailor their teaching strategies, leading to better academic performance. By collecting data on student performance and engagement, adaptive technologies help educators make informed decisions about how to further individualize learning content and methodologies. Continuous feedback loops inform both students and educators about progress, enabling timely interventions and adjustments to learning paths.

These tools are especially beneficial for students with diverse learning needs, including those with learning disabilities, by adapting content delivery to individual paces and needs. Assistive technologies, such as screen readers, speech-to-text tools, and alternative input devices, enhance accessibility for students with disabilities, ensuring inclusivity in digital learning. Adaptive technologies are particularly beneficial in subjects such as mathematics, languages, and sciences, where understanding builds progressively. These technologies support personalized learning by providing customized content that matches each student's learning curve.

Current research highlights how adaptive learning technologies support individual learning paths, enhance engagement, and improve academic achievement across various educational contexts. For instance, Demartini et al. (2024) found that students using AI-enhanced adaptive learning platforms showed significant improvements in various academic skills. These environments provide varied digital interactions, enhancing students' ability to navigate and utilize digital tools effectively, thus preparing them for a digital economy and independent learning. Similarly, Jadán-Guerrero et al. (2024) demonstrated that adaptive learning systems are particularly effective in inclusive settings, catering to students with diverse learning abilities and special needs. Their study observed that adaptive technologies could individualize learning experiences in real-time, making education more accessible and equitable. Furthermore, Er-radi et al. (2024) found that machine learning in adaptive online learning environments significantly enhanced learner engagement.

The personalized nature of learning and immediate feedback were key factors in increasing student engagement, which is crucial for long-term educational success. Additionally, these findings collectively underscore the importance of AI and adaptive technologies in tailoring educational content to meet individual student needs, thereby improving engagement and optimizing learning outcomes. Mejeh and Rehm (2024) demonstrate that integrating natural language processing (NLP) into adaptive learning enhances personalization, making education more responsive to individual needs. Güngören et al. (2024) highlight key trends in adaptive learning research, revealing a growing focus on AI integration for personalized learning experiences.

Ayeni et al. (2024) review AI's role in personalized learning, showing how tailored educational content can significantly improve academic performance and engagement. Judijanto et al. (2024) discuss the transformative potential of AI-based technologies in creating dynamic and interactive learning environments. These studies collectively reveal that adaptive learning technologies significantly enhance digital literacy and accommodate diverse educational needs. By incorporating insights from this robust body of research, educational stakeholders can better advocate for and implement these technologies, ensuring they are used optimally to meet modern education challenges. This evidence-based approach reinforces the value of adaptive learning technologies and guides future innovations in educational practice. The success of adaptive learning is further amplified when combined with other educational technologies, as illustrated in Table 3.8.

Table 3.8 outlines the roles and interactions of various educational technologies within the DIGICOMPASS framework, showing how they collectively create a personalized, inclusive, and adaptive learning environment by enhancing accessibility, engagement, and real-time feedback. Figure 3.2 complements this by visually mapping the intersections and compatibility of these technologies, highlighting their synergy and how they collaboratively support the overarching goals of DIGICOMPASS.

With insights into intersections and compatibilities, we can now explore the innovative and immersive educational experiences enabled by these integrations.

3.6 Enhanced Educational Experiences

The integration of diverse educational technologies within the DIGICOMPASS framework produces a range of enhanced educational experiences, each contributing to a comprehensive and adaptable learning

Table 3.8 Intersecting technologies in DIGICOMPASS

Technology type	Technologies and description	DIGICOMPASS integration	Intersections
Adaptive learning	*AI-powered learning platforms:* Use AI to personalize learning experiences based on student data, learning pace, and preferences	Tailors content to individual student needs, provides personalized feedback, and adjusts difficulty levels	Assistive, data analytics, immersive, gamification
	Machine learning algorithms: Analyze student interactions and adapt content in real-time to optimize learning outcomes	Dynamically adjusts learning paths and provides predictive insights for educators	

(*continued*)

Table 3.8 (continued)

Technology type	Technologies and description	DIGICOMPASS integration	Intersections
Assistive	*Screen readers:* Software that reads text aloud for students with visual impairments or reading difficulties	Enhances accessibility for students with disabilities, ensuring inclusivity in digital learning	Adaptive learning, collaborative, immersive
	Speech-to-text tools: Converts spoken words into text to assist students with writing difficulties or physical impairments	Supports students in completing assignments and participating in discussions	
	Alternative input devices: Devices such as adaptive keyboards or eye-tracking systems for students with physical disabilities	Enables all students to interact with digital content regardless of physical limitations	
Immersive	*Extended reality (XR):* Encompasses VR, AR, and MR, creating immersive digital environments and experiences	Provides immersive simulations, virtual field trips, and interactive learning experiences	Adaptive learning, assistive, collaborative
	Virtual reality (VR): Creates fully immersive, computer-generated environments for experiential learning	Provides immersive simulations and virtual field trips, enhancing engagement and experiential learning	
	Augmented reality (AR): Overlays digital information onto the real world, enhancing physical environments with interactive elements	Integrates interactive and contextual information into physical spaces, enriching learning experiences	
	Mixed reality (MR): Combines elements of both VR and AR, allowing real and virtual objects to interact	Facilitates interactive and immersive learning experiences that blend physical and digital worlds	

(*continued*)

Table 3.8 (continued)

Technology type	Technologies and description	DIGICOMPASS integration	Intersections
Collaborative	*Online collaboration platforms:* Tools like Google Workspace and Microsoft Teams that facilitate real-time collaboration among students	Enables students to work together on projects, share resources, and communicate effectively	Adaptive learning, assistive, immersive
	Interactive whiteboards: Digital boards that allow for interactive lessons and real-time collaboration in the classroom	Supports interactive teaching methods and enhances student engagement during lessons	
Data analytic	*Learning analytics dashboards:* Provide educators with insights into student performance and learning patterns	Helps educators make data-driven decisions to improve instructional strategies and student outcomes	Adaptive learning, content delivery, gamification
Content delivery	*E-learning platforms:* Comprehensive platforms that host and deliver educational content and resources online	Centralizes learning materials and provides students with flexible access to resources	Collaborative tools. data analytics
	Mobile learning apps: Educational applications designed for mobile devices, allowing learning on-the-go	Supports anytime, anywhere learning, accommodating the modern student's lifestyle	
Gamification	*Gamification technologies:* Incorporates game elements into learning to make educational content more engaging and enjoyable	Increases motivation and engagement, particularly for younger students or those needing additional encouragement	Adaptive learning, data analytics

environment. These experiences are transformative, offering personalized and engaging pathways for student growth and academic success. First, personalized learning is a cornerstone of this integration. AI-driven adaptive learning systems and personalized content delivery tailor educational material to the individual needs of each student, allowing learners to progress at their optimal pace and addressing unique strengths and areas for

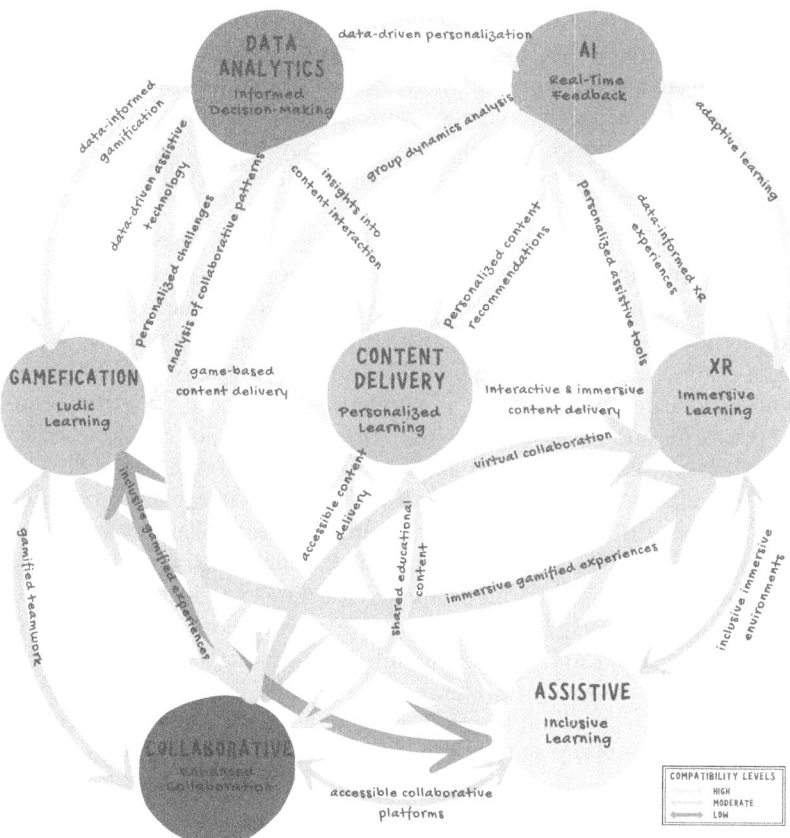

Fig. 3.2 Technological intersection and compatibility

improvement. Research by VanLehn (2011) and more recently by Laak and Aru (2024) supports the effectiveness of these personalized approaches in fostering deeper understanding and sustained academic growth.

Additionally, real-time feedback plays a crucial role in promoting a growth mindset among students. Continuous assessment and feedback from AI and data analytics tools provide immediate insights into student performance, helping them identify their strengths and areas needing improvement. This ongoing feedback loop encourages students to reflect on their learning processes and strive for continuous improvement, as highlighted by Pierce (2024). Enhanced accessibility ensures that all students, regardless of their abilities, can access and engage with learning materials effectively. AI-powered assistive tools and inclusive design features integrated into content delivery and XR platforms make educational resources more accessible, creating an equitable learning environment. Both real-time feedback and enhanced accessibility contribute to a more inclusive and effective learning environment, as emphasized by Sappaile et al. (2024).

Furthermore, immersive learning experiences, facilitated by XR technologies, offer lifelike, interactive environments that make complex subjects more tangible and engaging. These experiences enhance understanding and retention, providing students with a deeper connection to the material, as demonstrated by Lee et al. (2023) and Marougkas et al. (2024). In addition, collaborative learning is significantly enhanced with collaborative platforms and XR environments. These technologies enable seamless teamwork and communication among students, fostering essential skills such as collaboration, problem-solving, and effective communication. Laak and Aru (2024) highlight the benefits of these collaborative experiences in preparing students for real-world challenges. Moreover, increased engagement is achieved through gamified learning experiences and immersive XR environments. These tools make learning enjoyable, encouraging active participation and improving retention. Bacca et al. (2014) and James et al. (2024) provide evidence of the positive impact of gamification on student motivation and learning outcomes. Finally, informed decision-making is enhanced through data analytics, which provides educators with critical insights into student performance and engagement. This data-driven approach allows teachers to make informed decisions that enhance teaching strategies and learning outcomes, as underscored by Laak and Aru (2024).

In sum, the integration of AI, XR, and other educational technologies creates a comprehensive and adaptable learning environment. While AI and XR technologies are highly compatible and enhance each other, assistive, collaborative, gamification, data analytics, and content delivery technologies play crucial supporting roles. Together, they produce a multifaceted educational experience that is personalized, inclusive, immersive, and engaging. This synergy addresses diverse learning needs and prepares students for a technologically advanced and interconnected world. Although there are challenges in integrating technologies with low or moderate compatibility, the potential educational benefits make it worthwhile to pursue improvements. Ongoing research and development, coupled with technological advancements, are expected to enhance compatibility, making educational experiences more inclusive, engaging, and effective. Summarizing these insights, we conclude by reflecting on the broader implications of integrating personalized learning strategies and advanced technologies in education.

3.7 Conclusion

This chapter has outlined a comprehensive approach to integrating various technologies within an educational framework, emphasizing the importance of personalized learning. By leveraging adaptive learning technologies, educators can tailor educational experiences to individual student needs, thereby enhancing engagement, retention, and overall academic performance. The theoretical underpinnings of personalized learning, drawing on Constructivism, Vygotsky's Sociocultural Theory, Cognitive Load Theory, and Connectivism, create a robust and dynamic learning environment.

The integration of assistive technologies ensures inclusivity, making education accessible to all students. Immersive technologies provide engaging, experiential learning opportunities that deepen the understanding of complex concepts. Collaborative technologies foster teamwork and communication, while analytic and feedback tools enable continuous assessment and personalized instructional adjustments. Content delivery technologies offer flexible access to learning materials, and gamification technologies increase motivation and engagement through interactive and enjoyable learning experiences. Research supports the effectiveness of these technologies, demonstrating significant improvements in student engagement, motivation, and academic achievement. Studies show that adaptive learning systems are particularly effective in inclusive settings, catering to a wide range of learning abilities and special needs. This evidence-based approach underscores the value of adaptive learning technologies and guides future innovations in educational practice.

Reflecting on the broader implications, it becomes evident that integrating personalized learning strategies and advanced technologies within educational frameworks like DIGICOMPASS has transformative potential. Personalized learning not only addresses the unique needs of each student but also promotes a deeper connection to the material, fostering intrinsic motivation and a lifelong love of learning. The use of advanced technologies, from AI-driven adaptive systems to immersive XR environments, equips students with the skills necessary for navigating the complexities of a digital and interconnected world.

References

Akhiat, M. (2024). Second language acquisition in the era of technology and artificial intelligence: Exploring new frontiers. *DigitalCommons@USU*. https://digitalcommons.usu.edu/gradreports2023/28/

Ayeni, O. O., Al Hamad, N. M., Chisom, O. N., Osawaru, B., & Adewusi, O. E. (2024). AI in education: A review of personalized learning and educational technology. *GSC Advanced Research and Reviews, 18*(2), 261–271. https://gsconlinepress.com/journals/gscarr/sites/default/files/GSCARR-2024-0062.pdf

Bacca, J., Baldiris, S., Fabregat, R., Graf, S., & Kinshuk. (2014). Augmented reality trends in education: A systematic review of research and applications. *Educational Technology & Society, 17*(4), 133–149.

Barrot, J. S. (2024). ChatGPT as a language learning tool: An emerging technology report. *Technology, Knowledge and Learning, 29*(2), 1151–1156. https://www.researchgate.net/publication/376376372_ChatGPT_as_a_Language_Learning_Tool_An_Emerging_Technology_Report

Barsalou, L. W. (2008). Grounded cognition. *Annual Review of Psychology, 59*, 617–645.

Bruner, J. S. (1960). *The process of education*. Harvard University Press.

Bui, H. P., & Namaziandost, E. (2023). *Innovations in technologies for language teaching and learning*. Multilingual Matters.

Christanti, M. F., Mawangir, M., Arevin, A. T., Ramadhan, I., & Limijadi, E. K. S. (2024). The digital divide in education: Bridging gaps in the era of online learning. *Migration Letters, 21*(S4), 1070–1079.

Conrad, M., Kablitz, D., & Schumann, S. (2024). Learning effectiveness of immersive virtual reality in education and training: A systematic review of findings. *Computers & Education: X Reality, 4*, 100053. https://www.sciencedirect.com/science/article/pii/S2949678024000035

Demartini, C. G., Sciascia, L., Bosso, A., & Manuri, F. (2024). Artificial intelligence bringing improvements to adaptive learning in education: A case study. *Sustainability, 16*(1347). https://doi.org/10.3390/su16031347

Dewey, J. (1938). *Experience and education*. Kappa Delta Pi.

Ellis, N. C., & Wulff, S. (2014). Usage-based approaches to SLA. In B. VanPatten & J. Williams (Eds.), *Theories in second language acquisition: An introduction* (2nd ed., pp. 87–105). Routledge.

Eren, Ö. (2024). Towards multilingual turn in language classes: Plurilingual awareness as an indicator of intercultural communicative competence. *International Journal of Multilingualism, 21*(2), 783–801.

Er-radi, H., Touis, B., & Aammou, S. (2024). Machine learning in adaptive online learning for enhanced learner engagement. In *Technological tools for innovative teaching* (pp. 43–63). IGI Global.

European Commission, Directorate-General for Education, Youth, Sport and Culture. (2023). *Working group on schools (2021–25) "pathways to school success"*. Publications Office of the European Union. https://data.europa.eu/doi/10.2766/14836

Familoni, B. T., & Onyebuchi, N. C. (2024). Augmented and virtual reality in US education: A review: Analyzing the impact, effectiveness, and future prospects of AR/VR tools in enhancing learning experiences. *International Journal of Applied Research in Social Sciences, 6*(4), 642–663. https://fepbl.com/index.php/ijarss/article/view/1043

García, O., & Wei, L. (2014). *Translanguaging: Language, bilingualism and education*. Palgrave Macmillan.

González-Lloret, M., & Rock, K. (2022). Tasks in technology-mediated contexts. In N. Ziegler & M. González-Lloret (Eds.), *The Routledge handbook of second language acquisition and technology* (pp. 36–49). Routledge.

Güngören, Ö. C., Erdoğan, D. G., Çelik, N., Bilgin, S., & Köse, M. K. (2024). The trends in adaptive learning research: A bibliometric analysis study. *International Journal of Educational Research Review, 9*(3), 160–183.

Han, T., & Sari, E. (2024). An investigation on the use of automated feedback in Turkish EFL students' writing classes. *Computer Assisted Language Learning, 37*(4), 961–985.

Huang, X., Zou, D., Cheng, G., & Xie, H. (2021). A systematic review of AR and VR enhanced language learning. *Sustainability, 13*(9), 4639. https://doi.org/10.3390/su13094639

Huang, X., Zou, D., Cheng, G., Chen, X., & Xie, H. (2023). Trends, research issues and applications of artificial intelligence in language education. *Educational Technology & Society, 26*(1), 112–131. http://index.j-ets.net/Published/26_1/ETS_26_1_09.pdf

Jadán-Guerrero, J., Tamayo-Narvaez, K., Méndez, E., & Valenzuela, M. (2024). Adaptive learning environments: Integrating artificial intelligence for special education advances. In C. Stephanidis, M. Antona, S. Ntoa, & G. Salvendy (Eds.), *HCI international 2024 posters. HCII 2024. Communications in computer and information science* (Vol. 2117, pp. 86–94). Springer. https://doi.org/10.1007/978-3-031-61953-3_10

James, W., Oates, G., & Schonfeldt, N. (2024). Improving retention while enhancing student engagement and learning outcomes using gamified mobile technology. *Accounting Education*, 1–21. https://www.tandfonline.com/doi/pdf/10.1080/09639284.2024.2326009

Jeon, J. (2024). Exploring AI chatbot affordances in the EFL classroom: Young learners' experiences and perspectives. *Computer Assisted Language Learning, 37*(1–2), 1–26.

Jewitt, C., Bezemer, J., & O'Halloran, K. (2016). *Introducing multimodality*. Routledge.

Judijanto, L., Atsani, M. R., & Chadijah, S. (2024). Trends in the development of artificial intelligence-based technology in education. *International Journal of Teaching and Learning, 2*(6), 1722–1723. https://injotel.org/index.php/12/article/view/197/227

Kramsch, C. (2014). Teaching foreign languages in an era of globalization: Introduction. *Modern Language Journal, 98*(1), 296–311.

Krashen, S. D. (1985). *The input hypothesis: Issues and implications.* Longman.

Laak, K.-J., & Aru, J. (2024). AI and personalized learning: Bridging the gap with modern educational goals. ArXiv, 2404.02798 https://arxiv.org/pdf/2404.02798

Lantolf, J. P. (2000). *Sociocultural theory and second language learning.* Oxford University Press.

Lee, H., & Lee, J. H. (2024). The effects of AI-guided individualized language learning: A meta-analysis. *Language Learning & Technology, 28*(2), 134–162.

Lee, S. M., Yang, Z., & Wu, J. G. (2023). Live, play, and learn: Language learner engagement in the immersive VR environment. *Education and Information Technologies, 29*, 1–22.

Loewen, S., Isbell, D. R., & Sporn, Z. (2020). The effectiveness of app-based language instruction for developing receptive linguistic knowledge and oral communicative ability. *Foreign Language Annals, 53*(2), 226–249.

Long, M. H. (1996). The role of the linguistic environment in second language acquisition. In W. C. Ritchie & T. K. Bhatia (Eds.), *Handbook of second language acquisition* (pp. 413–468). Academic Press.

Mackey, A., Abbuhl, R., & Gass, S. M. (2013). Interactionist approach. In *The Routledge handbook of second language acquisition* (pp. 7–23). Routledge.

Marougkas, A., Troussas, C., Krouska, A., & Sgouropoulou, C. (2024). How personalized and effective is immersive virtual reality in education? A systematic literature review for the last decade. *Multimedia Tools and Applications, 83*(6), 18185–18233.

Mejeh, M., & Rehm, M. (2024). Taking adaptive learning in educational settings to the next level: Leveraging natural language processing for improved personalization. *Educational Technology Research and Development, 72*, 1597–1621. https://rdcu.be/d1TJE

Piaget, J. (1970). *Science of education and the psychology of the child.* Orion Press.

Pierce, K. (2024). AI-powered personalized feedback: Save time & spark critical minds. In *Artificial intelligence in education conference: Shaping future classrooms.* Ontario Tech University. https://ecampusontario.pressbooks.pub/artificialintelligenceineducationconference/chapter/ai-powered-personalized-feedback-save-time-spark-critical-minds/

Rezkilaturahmi, Madya, S., & Triastuti, A. (2024). Blended teaching of EFL listening and speaking in junior secondary school. In *Proceedings of the International Conference on Current Issues in Education (ICCIE 2023)* (pp. 13–19). Atlantis Press.

Sappaile, B. I., Vandika, A. Y., Deiniatur, M., Nuridayanti, N., & Arifudin, O. (2024). The role of artificial intelligence in the development of digital era educational progress. *Journal of Artificial Intelligence and Development*, *3*(1), 1–8.

Schorr, I., Plecher, D. A., Eichhorn, C., & Klinker, G. (2024). Foreign language learning using augmented reality environments: A systematic review. *Frontiers in Virtual Reality*, *5*, 1288824. https://doi.org/10.3389/frvir.2024.1288824

Siemens, G. (2005). Connectivism: A learning theory for the digital age. *International Journal of Instructional Technology and Distance Learning*, *2*(1), 3–10. https://edtechbooks.s3.us-west-2.amazonaws.com/pdfs/133/6849.pdf

Sung, M. C., & Kang, S. (2024). Developing AI chatbots for pragmatic instruction of Korean secondary L2 English learners. *Korean Journal of English Language and Linguistics*, *24*, 441–459.

Swain, M. (1985). Communicative competence: Some roles of comprehensible input and comprehensible output in its development. In S. Gass & C. Madden (Eds.), *Input in Second Language Acquisition* (pp. 235–253). Newbury House.

Sweller, J. (1988). Cognitive load during problem solving: Effects on learning. *Cognitive Science*, *12*(2), 257–285.

Tafazoli, D. (2024). Extended reality in computer-assisted language learning. In H. P. Bui & E. Namaziandost (Eds.), *Innovations in technologies for language teaching and learning. Studies in computational intelligence* (Vol. 1159, pp. 17–34). Springer. https://doi.org/10.1007/978-3-031-63447-5_2

Van Lier, L. (2004). *The ecology and semiotics of language learning: A sociocultural perspective*. Springer.

VanLehn, K. (2011). The relative effectiveness of human tutoring, intelligent tutoring systems, and other tutoring systems. *Educational Psychologist*, *46*(4), 197–221.

Vygotsky, L. S. (1978). *Mind in society: The development of higher psychological processes*. Harvard University Press.

Wang, M. L. C. (2024). Mobile mavericks: A twenty-year retrospective on advancements and challenges in language learning. *International Journal of Current Educational Practice*, *12*(2), 140–149. https://americaserial.com/Journals/index.php/IJCEP/article/view/1059/1248

Wei, L. (2018). Translanguaging as a practical theory of language. *Applied Linguistics*, *39*(1), 9–30.

Wei, L. (2023). Artificial intelligence in language instruction: Impact on English learning achievement, L2 motivation, and self-regulated learning. *Frontiers in Psychology*, *14*, 1261955. https://doi.org/10.3389/fpsyg.2023.1261955

Zhang, Z., & Huang, X. (2024). Exploring the impact of the adaptive gamified assessment on learners in blended learning. *Education and Information Technologies.*, *29*(16), 21869–21889. https://doi.org/10.1007/s10639-024-12708-w

CHAPTER 4

Unpacking Digital Literacies and Multiliteracies

Abstract This chapter discusses the foundational roles of digital literacies and multiliteracies within the DIGICOMPASS framework. Positioned as the guiding "North" of the compass, digital literacy is vital for thriving in an interconnected, digitized world, encompassing technical proficiency, critical thinking, ethical engagement, and multimodal communication. Multiliteracies expand on this by integrating text, audio, visual, and interactive media to foster global citizenship through cultural sensitivity, critical thinking, and ethical practices. Intercultural and plurilingual multiliteracy is highlighted as essential for navigating multilingual and multicultural contexts, enhancing linguistic proficiency and cultural understanding. The chapter underscores the importance of embedding these literacies into curricula to prepare students for challenges including communication, ethical engagement, and cultural adaptability. However, it also raises concerns about conceptual overload and the need for clear definitions.

Keywords Abilities • Competencies • Digital literacy • Multiliteracy • Skills

4.1 INTRODUCTION

This chapter delves into the foundational roles of digital literacies and multiliteracies within the DIGICOMPASS educational framework. As society becomes increasingly digitized and interconnected, the traditional concept of literacy—centered around reading and writing—has expanded to encompass a wide array of capabilities necessary for thriving in diverse and complex digital environments. In DIGICOMPASS, digital literacy represents the north of the metaphorical compass, serving as the guiding star that illuminates the path for all other literacies and multiliteracies. Digital literacy emerges as the most crucial of all literacies, providing the foundation upon which other skills, competencies, and abilities are built.

Digital literacy encompasses technical proficiency, critical thinking, ethical understanding, and the ability to navigate the vast amounts of information available online. By mastering digital literacy, students gain the essential tools to engage with and contribute to the digital world safely and effectively. Digital multiliteracies extend beyond digital literacy to include the ability to communicate and interpret meaning through multiple modes—text, audio, visual, and interactive media. This concept recognizes that digital communication involves a complex interplay of various media forms. Digital multiliteracies require students to be proficient in navigating and producing content across different platforms, fostering deeper engagement with diverse communication methods and cultural contexts. Integrating these multiliteracies within the DIGICOMPASS framework fosters global citizenship by promoting cultural sensitivity, ethical engagement, and critical thinking.

This chapter provides a comprehensive overview of how digital literacy serves as the cornerstone for developing a spectrum of multiliteracies within the DIGICOMPASS framework. By fostering these capabilities, DIGICOMPASS aims to prepare students for the complexities of a globalized and digitized world, ensuring they are equipped to become informed, ethical, and engaged global citizens.

4.2 Defining Literacies

Literacy typically meets the following criteria:

1. *Essential Skills:* These are specific, teachable tasks required to effectively navigate a particular domain, acquired through practice (Eshet-Alkalai, 2004; Ng, 2015; Gudmundsdottir & Hatlevik, 2018; Street, 2003). Such skills provide the foundational operational knowledge that supports all subsequent digital engagements.
2. *Critical Understanding:* This involves the ability to critically assess and evaluate information within a given domain. For example, evaluating the reliability of online sources is a key component of digital literacy (Ng, 2012).
3. *Contextual Application:* This refers to the practical use of skills and knowledge in real-world contexts. An example would be employing digital tools to complete a project or communicate effectively in digital spaces (Gee, 2015a).
4. *Ethical Awareness:* Understanding the ethical implications and responsibilities associated with actions in a particular domain is crucial. This includes respecting privacy and intellectual property rights in digital environments (Leu et al., 2013; O'Brien & Scharber, 2008).
5. *Holistic Competencies:* These go beyond task execution to encompass effective utilization in diverse scenarios. Competencies span all categories, embodying the understanding and strategies needed for the effective use of digital tools (Dede, 2010).
6. *Broader Abilities:* These include cognitive and practical aptitudes, such as critical thinking, evaluating sources, synthesizing information, and making informed decisions. They transcend skills and competencies, involving higher cognitive engagement and activities like ethical reasoning and cultural awareness (Jenkins & Ito, 2015).

Multiliteracy extends the concept of literacy to include proficiency in multiple modes of communication, such as visual, digital, and textual, recognizing the varied ways people make meaning in different contexts. Kress (2003) emphasizes that multiliteracy prepares students to navigate and interpret the diverse communication methods they encounter in the digital and globalized world. This concept is crucial as it acknowledges that communication today is not limited to text; it includes images, videos, and other multimedia elements that require distinct interpretative skills (Mills, 2015; Lotherington & Jenson, 2011).

The New London Group (1996) originally introduced the concept of multiliteracies, highlighting the need for flexible and dynamic literacy practices to meet the demands of a rapidly changing world. Their framework advocated for an expanded understanding of literacy that includes multiple modes of communication—visual, auditory, textual, and gestural. As digital technologies have evolved, so too has the framework. The integration of digital tools like multimedia, hypertext, and social media has significantly expanded the scope of multiliteracies. These tools have added new dimensions, necessitating skills in navigating and creating content in complex, multimodal environments.

Digital technologies have transformed the way meaning is made, shared, and interpreted. For example, multimedia content now requires students to engage with and create combinations of text, images, audio, and video. Hypertext introduces non-linear navigation, challenging the traditional sequential approach to reading and writing. Social media further complicates literacy by requiring proficiency in real-time, interactive, and often global communication. These developments demand a more sophisticated set of literacy practices, aligning with the New London Group's call for adaptability and creativity in literacy education.

Embracing multiliteracies is essential for developing students' abilities to operate in culturally diverse and digitally rich environments. They must be adept at understanding and creating content that transcends traditional boundaries (Cope & Kalantzis, 2015; Livingstone & Sefton-Green, 2016). This approach equips students to manage the complexities of a digital world and can be leveraged to promote social justice and equity in educational settings (Rowsell & Walsh, 2011; Sindoni & Moschini, 2021).

By recognizing the importance of multiliteracy, educators can better prepare students for the diverse communication challenges they will face. This comprehensive approach ensures that students are not only proficient in multiple forms of media but also capable of critical and creative thinking, ultimately fostering a more inclusive and equitable educational environment. As the landscape of communication continues to evolve, the New London Group's framework remains a vital foundation, now enriched and expanded by the integration of digital technologies.

4.3 THE IMPORTANCE OF DIGITAL LITERACY AS A MULTILITERACY

Digital literacy is fundamental in the twenty-first century. In today's interconnected world, it is as crucial as traditional literacies like reading, writing, and arithmetic. Education systems globally are increasingly integrating digital literacy into curricula from early schooling stages, ensuring that students understand how to use technological tools safely and effectively (UNESCO, 2018; OECD, 2023).

Digital literacy encompasses critical thinking skills necessary to navigate the vast amounts of information available online, including distinguishing between credible and non-credible sources, understanding digital footprints, and protecting personal data. As the global economy shifts toward knowledge-based industries, digital literacy becomes essential for students to compete in the global job market. Moreover, addressing the digital divide by providing equitable access to technology and high-quality digital education is crucial for ensuring that all students benefit from digital literacy (Cope & Kalantzis, 2015; Tinmaz et al., 2022).

Digital literacy should be considered a multiliteracy because it inherently involves multiple modes of communication and a range of interconnected skills necessary for effectively navigating the digital world. The traditional notion of literacy, which primarily focuses on reading and writing, has expanded to address the complexities of the digital age. Here are key reasons why digital literacy aligns with the concept of multiliteracy. Firstly, digital literacy requires proficiency in various forms of media, including text, audio, visual, and interactive content. This mirrors the essence of multiliteracy, which acknowledges that meaning is made through different modes and media. For example, a digitally literate individual must be able to interpret infographics, create videos, and engage with interactive platforms. The New London Group (1996) emphasized the need for literacy practices that go beyond traditional reading and writing to include multiple modes of communication, which aligns with the nature of digital literacy.

Furthermore, digital literacy encompasses a wide range of skills, such as technical proficiency, critical thinking, and ethical understanding. These skills are interconnected and overlap with other literacies, such as media literacy (understanding and creating media content) and information literacy (locating and evaluating information). This interconnectedness is a hallmark of multiliteracy, as discussed by Lankshear and Knobel (2008), who imply that digital literacy is not a singular entity but a collection of literacies involving multiple modes and media.

Additionally, as digital environments continually evolve, digital literacy requires dynamic and flexible literacy practices. This flexibility is central to the concept of multiliteracy, which emphasizes the need for adaptable literacy practices that can address the changing landscape of communication in the digital age. Even a quarter of a century ago, Cope and Kalantzis (2000) argued that literacy in the digital age involves diverse forms of meaning-making, suggesting that digital literacy is inherently a multiliteracy. This early recognition underscores the longstanding complexity and multifaceted nature of digital literacy, validating current educational approaches that integrate multiple literacies and emphasizing their enduring relevance in addressing the evolving digital landscape.

Moreover, digital literacy involves understanding the cultural and contextual nuances of digital communication. Engaging with global online communities requires sensitivity to cultural differences and the ability to communicate effectively across diverse contexts. This cultural awareness aligns with the principles of multiliteracy, which stress the importance of cultural and contextual factors in communication (Kress, 2003; Gee, 2015b).

Finally, digital literacy is not limited to passive consumption of information; it also involves active participation and content creation. This comprehensive engagement with digital content reflects the broader scope of multiliteracy, which includes producing, interacting with, and critically analyzing content across various digital platforms. Recognizing digital literacy as a multiliteracy allows for a more comprehensive understanding of the skills and competencies needed to thrive in a complex, digitized world.

4.4 Digital Literacies and Multiliteracies in DIGICOMPASS

DIGICOMPASS integrates digital literacies and multiliteracies across its four cardinal principles—digital literacy (North), inclusive practices (East), intercultural competence (South), and awareness of social strategies (West)—with global citizenship at the core.

- **Digital Literacy (North):** Equips students with the foundational skills required to navigate the digital world safely and effectively, including technical proficiency, critical thinking, and the ability to access, interpret, and engage with digital information (Eshet-Alkalai, 2004; Ng, 2012).
- **Inclusive Practices (East):** Ensures that education is accessible and equitable, promoting diversity and catering to various learning needs. Digital multiliteracies support this pillar by recognizing different forms of literacy beyond traditional reading and writing, including visual, digital, and media literacies (Cope & Kalantzis, 2015).
- **Intercultural Competence (South):** Fosters understanding and appreciation of diverse cultures, crucial for effective global citizenship. Digital multiliteracies enhance this pillar by integrating cultural and linguistic diversity into the curriculum, helping students navigate and interpret various cultural contexts, and enhancing their ability to communicate and collaborate across cultures (Byram, 2020; Jackson, 2018).
- **Awareness of Social Strategies (West):** Emphasizes ethical engagement and community growth, supported by digital multiliteracies that teach students the ethical implications of their digital actions and promote responsible digital citizenship. This includes understanding digital privacy, respecting intellectual property, and engaging positively in digital interactions (Ribble, 2015).
- **Global Citizenship (Core):** At the heart of DIGICOMPASS lies global citizenship, encompassing all four cardinal principles and aiming to prepare students to be informed, empathetic, and engaged global citizens. Digital multiliteracies underpin this concept by equipping students with the skills to engage effectively in a globalized world, fostering critical analysis of information, cross-cultural communication, and ethical participation in digital communities, ensuring students can navigate and contribute to the global digital landscape (New London Group, 1996; Spires et al., 2018).

In Chap. 3, the DIGICOMPASS framework integrates several key educational theories—Constructivism, Vygotsky's Sociocultural Theory, CLT, and Connectivism—to create a personalized, engaging, and effective learning environment. These theories collectively provide a robust foundation for developing digital literacies and multiliteracies, which are crucial for students in today's world.

Constructivism views learning as an active process where students build knowledge through practical experiences. This theory supports digital literacies by encouraging students to engage with digital tools and resources actively, fostering a deeper understanding through hands-on practice. By constructing their own learning pathways, students develop the ability to critically evaluate and use digital information effectively.

Vygotsky's Sociocultural Theory emphasizes the importance of social interactions and cultural contexts in learning. This perspective is integral to multiliteracies, which involve navigating and understanding diverse cultural and communicative practices. Through collaborative projects and interactions within digital platforms, students gain insights into different cultural perspectives, enhancing their intercultural competence and empathy.

CLT focuses on managing the cognitive demands placed on learners to optimize their learning experiences. By structuring digital content in ways that align with students' cognitive capacities, educators can prevent overload and ensure that learning is both effective and efficient. This theory is vital for digital literacies, as it guides the design of educational materials that facilitate comprehension and retention without overwhelming the learner.

Connectivism highlights the role of technological networks in learning, asserting that knowledge is distributed across a network of connections. This theory supports digital literacies by emphasizing the importance of building and navigating these networks to access and share information. In the DIGICOMPASS framework, connectivism encourages the use of digital tools to foster global connectivity and collaborative learning, preparing students to thrive in a networked world.

As technology evolves, so do the capabilities required to use it effectively. Digital multiliteracies ensure that students are not just consumers of technology but also proficient users who can leverage digital tools to enhance their learning, productivity, and creativity (Ng, 2012; Spires & Bartlett, 2012). These multiliteracies enable individuals to use technology for creation, communication, and problem-solving. Moreover, they involve critical thinking capabilities that enable students to evaluate the credibility and reliability of information found online, which is essential in an era where misinformation and fake news are prevalent (Wineburg et al., 2016; McGrew et al., 2017). These capabilities help individuals make informed decisions and avoid the pitfalls of misinformation.

Recognizing multiple literacies ensures that education is inclusive and responsive to diverse learning profiles, supporting students' varied strengths and preferences. A multiliteracies framework addresses cultural and linguistic diversity, fostering equitable and meaningful learning experiences. Multiliteracies prepare students to communicate across different cultural and linguistic contexts, which is increasingly important in a globalized world. By understanding and creating content in various modes, students enhance their ability to interact effectively with diverse audiences, strengthening their participation in global discourse (New London Group, 1996; Cope & Kalantzis, 2015). Embracing multiliteracies encourages students to think creatively and innovatively. They learn to produce content that combines text, images, video, and other media, which is a valuable skill in today's careers. Furthermore, teaching digital multiliteracies includes instilling an understanding of ethical behavior online. This involves respecting intellectual property, understanding digital privacy, and engaging in positive digital interactions (Ribble, 2015).

Digital literacies should be considered multiliteracies because they encompass a wide range of intersecting and overlapping capabilities. For example, mastering digital tools (TECHNOLOGY LITERACY) necessitates the ability to evaluate information (INFORMATION LITERACY), which in turn involves understanding online safety (CYBER SAFETY LITERACY). These literacies are not isolated but integrated, reflecting the complex and multifaceted nature of digital engagement. The ability to navigate digital environments, create content, and communicate effectively involves a combination of various literacies, making them inherently multiliteracies. While there are multiliteracies that are not inherently digital, within the DIGICOMPASS framework, digital literacy serves as a foundational component. Therefore, all the multiliteracies within this framework include a digital aspect, ensuring that students are equipped to thrive in an increasingly digitized world. Table 4.1 outlines the spectrum of digital multiliteracies in DIGICOMPASS, detailing the associated capabilities, applications, technologies, and learning outcomes.

Table 4.1 Spectrum of digital multiliteracies in DIGICOMPASS

Multiliteracy	Skills/competencies/abilities	Applications	Technologies	Learning outcomes
Digital (Eshet-Alkalai, 2004; Livingstone & Sefton-Green, 2016)	Mastering digital tools, evaluating information, understanding online safety, managing screen time, understanding the impact of digital media on mental health	Integrated tech workshops and projects, digital well-being workshops, mindfulness and technology integration activities	Office suites, graphic design software, safe browsing tools, screen time tracking apps, digital well-being platforms, mindfulness apps	Proficiency in digital tools, critical information evaluation, cybersecurity awareness, awareness of digital well-being, ability to manage digital consumption healthily
Intercultural and plurilingual (Coste et al., 2009; Gee, 2015b)	Enhancing digital communication, navigating cultural nuances, utilizing multiple communication modes, communicating across multiple languages	Collaborative projects and cultural exchanges	Google Workspace, video conferencing tools, cultural simulation software, language learning apps	Improved digital communication, intercultural sensitivity, multilingual proficiency, and collaborative skills
Ethical and critical (Jenkins & Ito, 2015; boyd, 2007)	Practicing ethical behavior, analyzing media, critical thinking, managing digital identity, understanding digital footprints	Interactive ethics and media analysis modules, digital identity workshops	Media education platforms, media critique tools, ethical decision-making simulations, privacy settings tools	Ethical digital conduct, media critique skills, understanding societal impacts, awareness of digital footprints

(*continued*)

Table 4.1 (continued)

Multiliteracy	Skills/ competencies/ abilities	Applications	Technologies	Learning outcomes
Creative and innovative (Lankshear & Knobel, 2008; Wing, 2006)	Creating digital content, innovating with technologies, understanding programming concepts, developing computational thinking	Creative content creation and innovation labs, coding bootcamps	Adobe Creative Cloud, interactive design tools (Figma, Canva), AI-driven design assistance, programming languages (Python, JavaScript), coding platforms (Scratch, Code.org)	Skills in visual communication, digital design principles, creativity and innovation, proficiency in coding, enhanced problem-solving abilities
Global and environmental (Bourn, 2014; Schield, 2004)	Understanding global issues, mastering sustainability practices, interpreting and using data effectively	Model United Nations simulations, eco-friendly projects, data analysis projects	Geographic information systems, environmental education platforms, spreadsheet software, data visualization tools, statistical analysis platforms	Nuanced understanding of international relations, commitment to environmental stewardship, proficiency in analyzing and presenting data, making data-driven decisions
Financial and economic (Lusardi & Mitchell, 2014; Schield, 2004)	Managing finances, understanding economic frameworks, analyzing data for financial decision-making	Stock market simulations, financial decision-making projects, data visualization tasks	Financial education tools, market simulation platforms, data visualization tools	Financial decision-making skills, economic literacy, proficiency in data analysis for financial purposes
Human rights and advocacy (Tibbitts, 2002)	Advocating for human rights, understanding equality	Role-playing scenarios on rights issues	Human rights education platforms	Awareness of human rights, advocacy skills

Digital multiliteracies ensure that students are equipped to handle everyday digital tasks safely and efficiently by integrating multiple modes of communication and cultural contexts. This includes proficiency in using multimedia, social platforms, and other digital communication tools in culturally sensitive ways. Such capabilities are essential for students to effectively engage in digital environments continually shaped by diverse cultural norms and languages, thereby enriching their global and intercultural engagement (Kress, 2003; Byram, 2020; Coste et al., 2009).

For instance, the global and environmental multiliteracy is woven into global studies modules where students explore international issues and geopolitical dynamics through activities like Model United Nations and global issue debates. These activities, supported by tools like Google Earth and World101, develop students' understanding of international relations and global citizenship (Nye, 2004). Additionally, environmental literacy is integrated through curricula emphasizing sustainability and ecological systems, where students use tools like Eco-Schools and National Geographic Kids for local environmental audits and digital ecological simulations, fostering a commitment to environmental stewardship (Lupton, 2014).

Similarly, financial and economic multiliteracy is taught within economics and mathematics courses, focusing on personal finance and budgeting. Simulations like those provided by EverFi and MarketWatch help students manage personal finances and understand economic principles (Association of College & Research Libraries, 2016). In parallel, human rights and advocacy multiliteracy is embedded in social studies and civics courses, exploring civil rights and international law through role-playing and collaborative projects. These are supported by tools like Amnesty International Education and Human Rights Watch, enhancing students' understanding of justice and advocacy (Shapiro & Stefkovich, 2016).

Furthermore, ethical and critical multiliteracy involves practicing ethical behavior, analyzing media, critical thinking, and managing digital identity. This includes understanding digital footprints and is facilitated by interactive ethics and media analysis modules, and digital identity workshops using media education platforms and privacy settings tools (Jenkins & Ito, 2015; boyd, 2007). Likewise, intercultural and plurilingual multiliteracy, which is linked to one of the DIGICOMPASS cardinal points/pillars—intercultural competence—focuses on enhancing digital communication, navigating cultural nuances, utilizing multiple communication modes, and communicating across multiple languages through collaborative projects and cultural exchanges using Google Workspace, video conferencing tools, and language learning apps (Gee, 2015b). This multiliteracy will be dealt with in the next section.

In addition, creative and innovative multiliteracy includes creating digital content, innovating with technologies, understanding programming concepts, and developing computational thinking. This is implemented through creative content creation and innovation labs, and coding bootcamps using Adobe Creative Cloud, prototyping tools, and programming languages like Python and JavaScript (Lankshear & Knobel, 2008; Wing, 2006). Furthermore, digital multiliteracy encompasses mastering digital tools, evaluating information, understanding online safety, managing screen time, and understanding the impact of digital media on mental health. This is achieved through integrated tech workshops and projects, digital well-being workshops, and mindfulness and technology integration activities (Eshet-Alkalai, 2004; Livingstone & Sefton-Green, 2016).

Embedding these multiliteracies into DIGICOMPASS ensures that students are active, informed, and responsible participants in the digital realm. This is crucial for fostering ethical participation, cultural understanding, and civic engagement—hallmarks of global citizenship (Westheimer & Kahne, 2004). Ethical technology use, a cornerstone of digital multiliteracies, involves understanding the social and cultural implications of online activities. It is imperative that students maintain a digital presence reflecting global stewardship values such as respect, privacy, and integrity (Ribble, 2015; Park, 2013).

Moreover, digital tools have transformed civic participation, offering platforms for advocacy and engagement. Students learn to leverage these tools, such as Slack and Microsoft Teams, to amplify their voices and influence societal change, stepping into roles of advocacy and leadership (Jenkins, 2009). Communication across cultures through digital channels, facilitated by digital multiliteracies, equips students with skills to navigate complex global discourses. This blending of cultural understanding with digital communication skills is critical for meaningful participation in global conversations (Keyton et al., 2013; Ting-Toomey & Chung, 2021).

Finally, an integral aspect of digital multiliteracies is understanding privacy and security. Educating students on navigating privacy settings and understanding data security practices ensures they are prepared to safeguard their digital identities (Park, 2013). By integrating a broad spectrum of digital multiliteracies, DIGICOMPASS enhances capabilities, enabling students to manage diverse digital interactions and engage in ethical, informed, and culturally sensitive ways (Spires et al., 2018). As these multiliteracies become increasingly essential, they shape how individuals interact with the world, influencing personal development and global interactions, ultimately fostering a more informed, ethical, and interconnected global community (Cope & Kalantzis, 2015).

4.4.1 Intercultural and Plurilingual Multiliteracy

Within the DIGICOMPASS framework, intercultural and plurilingual multiliteracy has emerged as essential for preparing students to navigate a globalized and digitized world. This approach emphasizes the incorporation of multiple languages and cultural contexts, recognizing the dynamic interplay between linguistic proficiency, intercultural awareness, and digital literacy.

Language learning today is profoundly influenced by digital tools and platforms, such as online courses, language learning apps like Duolingo and Babbel, virtual classrooms, and interactive games. These technologies foster digital literacy by requiring learners to engage with digital interfaces and navigate various software functionalities. Effective language learning also encompasses media literacy, as learners interact with content across diverse media types—text, video, and audio. This interaction is crucial in understanding context, cultural nuances, and non-verbal cues, which are vital in mastering a new language (Sundqvist & Sylvén, 2016). Language learning platforms often incorporate multimedia elements that enhance understanding and provide rich, contextual learning experiences. Additionally, information literacy is developed as language learners frequently engage in researching cultural contexts, synonyms, and grammar rules (Reinders & White, 2016). The use of various technologies to support language learning enhances technological fluency, expanding learners' technical skills and comfort with new technologies (Jenkins, 2009; Godwin-Jones, 2024).

Intercultural and plurilingual multiliteracy refers to the ability to use and understand multiple languages fluidly and effectively while navigating various cultural contexts. This concept acknowledges the complex and interconnected nature of language use in multicultural environments. García (2011) explores this in her comprehensive examination of bilingual education, highlighting the need for educational practices that support and develop intercultural and plurilingual competence. Coste et al. (2009)

provide a foundational framework for understanding plurilingual and pluricultural competence, discussing not only linguistic skills but also cultural understanding and the ability to switch between languages and cultural contexts depending on the situation. These competencies involve recognizing the value of multiple languages and cultural perspectives in educational practices, fostering a more holistic approach to language learning.

As educational practices continue to evolve, one concept closely related to intercultural and plurilingual multiliteracy that has gained prominence is translanguaging. Translanguaging involves using multiple languages interchangeably to enhance communication and learning. The CEFR defines translanguaging as "an action undertaken by plurilingual persons, where more than one language may be involved. A host of similar expressions now exist, but all are encompassed by the term plurilingualism" (CEFR, 2020, p. 31). García and Wei (2014) provide a theoretical basis for translanguaging, showing how it can be applied in educational settings to support students' linguistic and cognitive development. This practice encourages learners to draw on their entire linguistic repertoire, fostering a more holistic and inclusive approach to language education.

While both translanguaging and plurilingualism promote the use of multiple languages, there are distinct differences between the two. Plurilingualism generally refers to an individual's ability to use and switch between multiple languages as separate systems, each with its own grammar, vocabulary, and cultural nuances. It emphasizes the structured learning and use of languages in different contexts, promoting cultural and linguistic competence in each language individually (Coste et al., 2009). For example, a plurilingual person might speak English at work, French with family, and Spanish with friends, maintaining boundaries between these languages.

In contrast, translanguaging views the linguistic repertoire as a unified whole rather than separate languages. It involves blending and mixing languages within a single communicative act, reflecting how multilingual individuals naturally use their language skills fluidly and dynamically. This approach recognizes that multilingual speakers do not compartmentalize their languages but use them interchangeably to maximize communication and understanding (García & Wei, 2014). For instance, a student might start a sentence in one language and finish it in another or mix vocabulary from different languages in casual conversation. García and Otheguy (2020) further discuss the commonalities and divergences between plurilingualism and translanguaging, highlighting that while both concepts aim to enhance linguistic competence, translanguaging emphasizes the seamless integration of languages in practice.

Despite these differences, both concepts share the goal of fostering linguistic and intercultural competence. Translanguaging and plurilingualism both enhance learners' ability to navigate and thrive in multilingual and multicultural environments. They promote cognitive flexibility, critical thinking, and cultural sensitivity, essential skills in today's globalized world. Moreover, both approaches recognize the value of learners' entire linguistic repertoire and encourage educational practices that support multilingualism and cultural diversity.

Intercultural and plurilingual multiliteracy enhances an individual's capacity to operate within multilingual and multicultural digital contexts, enriching digital multiliteracies in various ways. Plurilingual individuals can navigate and bridge communication gaps across different language groups on digital platforms, enhancing both personal and professional interactions. Interacting with digital content in multiple languages boosts cultural understanding and sensitivity, which are key for effective global citizenship in digital realms. Intercultural and plurilingual multiliteracy also allows for a more nuanced critique of media, as individuals understand and interpret media content from multiple linguistic and cultural perspectives. Moreover, plurilingual learners are typically more adaptable to the dynamic nature of digital environments, ready to learn new tools and navigate changes in digital communication modes. The regular use of language learning technologies contributes to a higher level of comfort with digital tools, which is integral for thriving in technologically driven spaces (Coste et al., 2009; Godwin-Jones, 2024; García & Lin, 2017).

Multiliteracy extends the concept of literacy beyond traditional reading and writing to include digital, media, and visual literacies. Cope and Kalantzis (2015) advocate for a pedagogy of multiliteracies, emphasizing the importance of diverse forms of communication in contemporary education. Their framework integrates multiple literacies, preparing students to engage with a variety of media and cultural contexts. This approach aligns with the foundational work of the New London Group (1996), which introduced the concept of multiliteracies to address the changing landscape of communication in the digital age. Lütge (2022) expands on these ideas, discussing how digital media and multimodal texts can be leveraged to develop both intercultural and plurilingual multiliteracy.

The integration of these literacies is crucial for helping students navigate and create content across different platforms and cultural contexts.

This comprehensive approach ensures that learners are not only proficient in multiple languages but also skilled in using various forms of media to communicate effectively. Incorporating intercultural and plurilingual multiliteracy into educational frameworks like DIGICOMPASS involves recognizing the interconnectedness of language and media. This means designing curricula that support the development of linguistic skills alongside digital and media literacy. For instance, students might engage in digital storytelling projects that require them to use multiple languages and integrate text, images, and audio. Such projects not only enhance language proficiency but also foster critical thinking and creativity. Furthermore, the integration of these multiliteracies promotes cultural sensitivity and empathy. By engaging with diverse languages and media, students develop a deeper understanding of different cultural perspectives. This is essential for fostering global citizenship and preparing learners to participate in a multicultural and interconnected world. As García (2011) and Coste et al. (2009) emphasize, developing intercultural and plurilingual competence is key to effective communication and collaboration in global contexts.

4.5 Balancing Necessities and Criticisms

The expansion of literacy to encompass literacies and multiliteracies is crucial for modern education. However, it is important to address the criticisms and challenges associated with this broader concept. While some critics argue that this expansion risks conceptual overload and dilutes the meaning of literacy, the integration of multiliteracies into the DIGICOMPASS framework is both intentional and justified.

One primary criticism is the risk of conceptual overload. The term "literacy" has been extended to include a wide array of skills, competencies, and abilities, leading to concerns that its meaning is becoming diluted. Street (2003) points out that while recognizing the ideological nature of literacy practices is valuable, the proliferation of specific literacies tied to particular social contexts can complicate the development of cohesive educational strategies. Despite these concerns, the modern world demands a diverse set of skills that extend beyond traditional literacies. Digital multiliteracies equip students to navigate, engage, and effectively communicate in a digitally interconnected landscape, which is essential for contemporary education (Leu et al., 2013; Belshaw, 2014).

Another concern is the lack of precision and clarity in literacy definitions. With so many literacies being recognized, it can become challenging to define what literacy education should specifically aim to achieve. This vagueness can complicate the development of targeted educational policies and curricula. Critics argue that foundational skills like reading and writing should not be overshadowed by additional competencies. However, DIGICOMPASS maintains a balanced approach by incorporating these new literacies alongside traditional ones. This ensures students are proficient in reading and writing while also being adept at using digital tools and understanding complex multimedia content (Ng, 2012; Spires et al., 2018).

Cultural and contextual variability is another challenge. The definition and relevance of literacy can vary significantly across different cultural and social contexts, making it difficult to establish universal standards. The New Literacy Studies (NLS) approach emphasizes the cultural and contextual nature of literacy practices, highlighting the need for flexible and context-sensitive educational approaches (Street, 2003, 2014). By integrating multiliteracies, DIGICOMPASS ensures that students are proficient in digital tools and capable of navigating and interpreting diverse cultural contexts. This cultural competence is crucial for effective global citizenship and international collaboration (Cope & Kalantzis, 2015).

Economic and political influences on literacy priorities also draw criticism. The current emphasis on digital literacy is often driven by the needs of a technology-driven economy. While this influence is undeniable, it does not diminish the importance of digital literacy. Navigating and leveraging digital tools is essential for economic participation and competitiveness in the global job market. Addressing the digital divide by providing equitable access to technology and high-quality digital education further ensures that all students benefit, promoting social equity (UNESCO, 2018; Warschauer & Matuchniak, 2010).

Practical implementation of a broad range of literacies in educational settings can be challenging. Educators may struggle to balance teaching multiple literacies within existing curricula and resources. However, these challenges can be addressed through careful planning, adequate training, and sufficient resources. The benefits of preparing students for the demands of the digital age far outweigh these logistical concerns. A comprehensive literacy education equips students with the skills needed to adapt to rapidly changing digital environments, engage meaningfully in global conversations, and contribute to society as informed, empathetic, and engaged global citizens (Gee, 2015a; Jenkins, 2009). In summary, integrating digital multiliteracies within the DIGICOMPASS framework is essential for preparing students to thrive in a complex, digital world, fostering critical thinking, cultural awareness, and ethical digital citizenship.

4.6 Conclusion

This chapter explores the essential roles of digital literacies and multiliteracies in contemporary education. It emphasizes that digital literacy, which involves the ability to find, evaluate, utilize, share, and create content using information technologies, is as fundamental as traditional literacy skills like reading and writing. The chapter argues that digital literacy serves as the cornerstone for other literacies, providing students with critical technical proficiency, ethical understanding, and the ability to navigate the vast digital landscape. Additionally, digital multiliteracies extend this foundation by incorporating multiple modes of communication, recognizing that digital communication today involves a complex interplay of text, audio, visual, and interactive media. This comprehensive approach ensures that students are not just consumers of technology but also proficient users who can leverage digital tools to enhance their learning, productivity, and creativity.

Furthermore, the chapter highlights the importance of integrating multiliteracies within the educational curriculum to promote global citizenship. By incorporating diverse literacies such as plurilingual literacy, media literacy, and information literacy, the DIGICOMPASS framework fosters cultural sensitivity, ethical engagement, and critical thinking. This integration prepares students to navigate and interpret various cultural contexts, enabling them to communicate and collaborate across different cultural and linguistic boundaries. Finally, this chapter underscores the need for education systems to adapt and expand their literacy definitions and practices to meet the evolving demands of society, ensuring that students become informed, ethical, and engaged global citizens.

References

Association of College & Research Libraries. (2016). *Framework for information literacy for higher education.* https://www.ala.org/acrl/standards/ilframework
Belshaw, D. (2014). *The essential elements of digital literacies.* https://dougbelshaw.com/essential-elements-book.pdf
Bourn, D. (2014). *The theory and practice of development education: A pedagogy for global social justice.* Routledge.
boyd, d. (2007). Why youth (heart) social network sites: The role of networked publics in teenage social life. In D. Buckingham (Ed.), *MacArthur foundation series on digital learning: youth, identity, and media volume* (pp. 119–142). MIT Press.
Byram, M. (2020). *Teaching and assessing intercultural communicative competence: Revisited.* Multilingual Matters.
Cope, B., & Kalantzis, M. (2000). Multiliteracies: The beginning of an idea. In B. Cope & M. Kalantzis (Eds.), *Multiliteracies: Literacy learning and the design of social futures* (pp. 3–8). Routledge.
Cope, B., & Kalantzis, M. (2015). *A pedagogy of multiliteracies: Learning by design.* Palgrave Macmillan.
Coste, D., Moore, D., & Zarate, G. (2009). *Plurilingual and pluricultural competence.* Council of Europe.
Council of Europe. (2020). *Common European Framework of Reference for Languages: Learning, Teaching, Assessment—Companion Volume.* Council of Europe. https://rm.coe.int/common-european-framework-of-reference-for-languages-learning-teaching/16809ea0d4
Dede, C. (2010). Comparing frameworks for 21st century skills. In J. Bellance & R. Brandt (Eds.), *21st century skills: Rethinking how students learn* (pp. 51–76). Solution Tree Press.
Eshet-Alkalai, Y. (2004). Digital literacy: A conceptual framework for survival skills in the digital era. *Journal of Educational Multimedia and Hypermedia, 13*(1), 93–106.
García, O. (2011). *Bilingual education in the 21st century: A global perspective.* Wiley.
García, O., & Lin, A. M. (2017). Translanguaging in bilingual education. In O. García, A. Lin, & S. May (Eds.), *Bilingual and multilingual education. Encyclopedia of language and education* (pp. 117–130). Springer.
García, O., & Otheguy, R. (2020). Plurilingualism and translanguaging: Commonalities and divergences. *International Journal of Bilingual Education and Bilingualism, 23*(1), 17–35.
García, O., & Wei, L. (2014). *Translanguaging: Language, bilingualism and education.* Palgrave Macmillan.
Gee, J. P. (2015a). *Literacy and education.* Routledge.

Gee, J. (2015b). *Social linguistics and literacies: Ideology in discourses* (5th ed.). Routledge.

Godwin-Jones, R. (2024). Distributed agency in second language learning and teaching through generative AI. *Language Learning & Technology, 28*(2), 5–30. https://www.lltjournal.org/item/10125-73570/

Gudmundsdottir, G. B., & Hatlevik, O. E. (2018). Newly qualified teachers' professional digital competence: Implications for teacher education. *European Journal of Teacher Education, 41*(2), 214–231. https://doi.org/10.1080/02619768.2017.1416085

Jackson, J. (2018). *Interculturality in international education*. Routledge.

Jenkins, H. (2009). *Confronting the challenges of participatory culture: Media education for the 21st century*. MIT Press.

Jenkins, H., & Ito, M. (2015). *Participatory culture in a networked era: A conversation on youth, learning, commerce, and politics*. Polity.

Keyton, J., Caputo, J. M., Ford, E. A., Fu, R., Leibowitz, S. A., Liu, T., Polasik, S. S., Ghosh, P., & Wu, C. (2013). Investigating verbal workplace communication behaviors. *The Journal of Business Communication, 50*(2), 152–169.

Kress, G. (2003). *Literacy in the new media age*. Routledge.

Lankshear, C., & Knobel, M. (2008). *Digital literacies: Concepts, policies and practices*. Peter Lang.

Leu, D. J., Kinzer, C. K., Coiro, J., Castek, J., & Henry, L. A. (2013). New literacies: A dual-level theory of the changing nature of literacy, instruction, and assessment. In D. E. Alvermann, N. J. Unrau, & R. B. Ruddell (Eds.), *Theoretical models and processes of literacy* (6th ed., pp. 1150–1181). International Reading Association.

Livingstone, S., & Sefton-Green, J. (2016). *The class: Living and learning in the digital age*. NYU Press.

Lotherington, H., & Jenson, J. (2011). Teaching multimodal and digital literacy in L2 settings: New literacies, new basics, new pedagogies. *Annual Review of Applied Linguistics, 31*, 226–246.

Lupton, E. (2014). *Graphic design thinking: Beyond brainstorming*. Princeton Architectural Press.

Lusardi, A., & Mitchell, O. S. (2014). The economic importance of financial literacy: Theory and evidence. *Journal of Economic Literature, 52*(1), 5–44.

Lütge, C. (Ed.). (2022). *Foreign language learning in the digital age: Theory and pedagogy for developing literacies*. Taylor & Francis.

McGrew, S., Ortega, T., Breakstone, J., & Wineburg, S. (2017). The challenge that's bigger than fake news: Civic reasoning in a social media environment. *American Educator, 41*(3), 4. https://files.eric.ed.gov/fulltext/EJ1156387.pdf

Mills, K. A. (2015). *Literacy theories for the digital age: Social, critical, multimodal, spatial, material and sensory lenses*. Multilingual Matters.

New London Group. (1996). A pedagogy of multiliteracies: Designing social futures. *Harvard Educational Review, 66*(1), 60–92.

Ng, W. (2012). Can we teach digital natives digital literacy? *Computers & Education, 59*(3), 1065–1078.

Ng, W. (2015). *New digital technology in education: Conceptualizing professional learning for educators*. Springer.

Nye, J. S. (2004). *Soft power: The means to success in world politics*. PublicAffairs.

O'Brien, D., & Scharber, C. (2008). Digital literacies go to school: Potholes and possibilities. *Journal of Adolescent & Adult Literacy, 62*(2), 119–123.

OECD. (2023). *OECD digital education outlook 2023: Towards an effective digital education ecosystem*. OECD Publishing. https://doi.org/10.1787/c74f03de-en

Park, Y. J. (2013). Digital literacy and privacy behavior online. *Communication Research, 40*(2), 215–236.

Reinders, H., & White, C. (2016). 20 years of autonomy and technology: How far have we come and where to next? *Language Learning & Technology, 20*(2), 143–154.

Ribble, M. (2015). *Digital citizenship in schools: Nine elements all students should know*. International Society for Technology in Education.

Rowsell, J., & Walsh, M. (2011). Rethinking literacy education in new times: Multimodality, multiliteracies & new literacies. *Brock Education: A Journal of Educational Research and Practice, 21*, 53–62.

Schield, M. (2004). Information literacy, statistical literacy, data literacy. *IASSIST Quarterly, 28*(2/3), 6–11.

Shapiro, J. P., & Stefkovich, J. A. (2016). *Ethical leadership and decision making in education: Applying theoretical perspectives to complex dilemmas*. Routledge.

Sindoni, M. G., & Moschini, I. (Eds.). (2021). *Multimodal literacies across digital learning contexts*. Taylor & Francis.

Spires, H. A., & Bartlett, M. E. (2012). *Digital literacies and learning: Designing a path forward* (Friday Institute White Paper Series). North Carolina State University.

Spires, H. A., Paul, C. M., & Kerkhoff, S. N. (2018). Digital literacy for the 21st century. In *Encyclopedia of Information Science and Technology* (4th ed., pp. 2235–2242). IGI Global.

Street, B. V. (2003). What's "new" in new literacy studies? Critical approaches to literacy in theory and practice. *Current Issues in Comparative Education, 5*(2), 77–91.

Street, B. V. (2014). *Social literacies: Critical approaches to literacy in development, ethnography and education*. Routledge.

Sundqvist, P., & Sylvén, L. K. (2016). *Extramural English in teaching and learning: From theory and research to practice*. Palgrave Macmillan.

Tibbitts, F. (2002). Understanding what we do: Emerging models for human rights education. *International Review of Education, 48*(3–4), 159–171.

Ting-Toomey, S., & Chung, L. C. (2021). *Understanding intercultural communication*. Oxford University Press.

Tinmaz, H., Lee, Y. T., Fanea-Ivanovici, M., & Baber, H. (2022). A systematic review on digital literacy. *Smart Learning Environments, 9*(1), 21. https://doi.org/10.1186/s40561-022-00204-y

UNESCO. (2018). *A global framework of reference on digital literacy skills for indicator 4.4.2*. UNESCO Institute for Statistics. https://uis.unesco.org/sites/default/files/documents/ip51-global-framework-reference-digital-literacy-skills-2018-en.pdf

Warschauer, M., & Matuchniak, T. (2010). New technology and digital worlds: Analyzing evidence of equity in access, use, and outcomes. *Review of Research in Education, 34*(1), 179–225.

Westheimer, J., & Kahne, J. (2004). What kind of citizen? The politics of educating for democracy. *American Educational Research Journal, 41*(2), 237–269.

Wineburg, S., McGrew, S., Breakstone, J., & Ortega, T. (2016). *Evaluating information: The cornerstone of civic online reasoning*. Stanford Digital Repository. https://purl.stanford.edu/fv751yt5934

Wing, J. M. (2006). Computational thinking. *Communications of the ACM, 49*(3), 33–35.

CHAPTER 5

Implementing DIGICOMPASS for the Global Citizen

Abstract This chapter presents strategies for implementing the DIGICOMPASS framework, highlighting its alignment with national and supranational standards, including the UN Sustainable Development Goals, Common European Framework of Reference for Languages, and International Baccalaureate. A phased implementation approach ensures flexibility and scalability, incorporating curriculum mapping, pilot programs, and iterative refinement. Strategic solutions for inclusivity emphasize accessibility through device compatibility, multilingual content, and culturally responsive materials. Partnerships with community organizations and NGOs help address resource gaps, while investments in digital infrastructure and assistive technologies ensure equitable access. Professional development is central to this process, equipping educators with advanced digital tools, collaborative strategies, and sustained support through workshops, mentoring, and professional learning communities. DIGICOMPASS integrates mixed-method evaluations, real-time feedback, and adaptive technologies to assess student outcomes and curriculum impact, capturing the dynamic relationship between learning and teaching.

Keywords Curriculum mapping · Framework alignment · Inclusivity and accessibility · Mixed-methods assessment · Professional development

5.1 Introduction

This chapter outlines strategies for transforming the DIGICOMPASS framework into a comprehensive curriculum that fosters global citizenship. By aligning with national educational standards, supranational frameworks, and global objectives, DIGICOMPASS ensures its relevance and adaptability across diverse educational settings. Its flexible design allows it to address specific local challenges while leveraging global strengths. Central to strategic implementation is the role of professional development in empowering educators to integrate and implement the curriculum effectively using advanced digital tools and innovative pedagogical strategies. The chapter also highlights a phased integration approach, ensuring careful planning, continuous improvement, and scalability. By embedding continuous assessment and feedback, DIGICOMPASS remains responsive to the evolving needs of education, supporting accessibility, cultural relevance, and emotional well-being.

5.2 Strategic Integration

To achieve effective global implementation, DIGICOMPASS aligns with national educational standards, international frameworks, and global objectives. Initially, the framework focuses on a dozen English-speaking countries, leveraging consistency in language and educational systems for straightforward analysis. This targeted approach lays a solid foundation for broader expansion into diverse educational contexts.

As outlined in Sect. 5.2.1, DIGICOMPASS's adaptability is evident in its compatibility with various national curricula, demonstrating that its core principles of digital literacy, global citizenship, and intercultural competence are embraced by policymakers worldwide. However, effective implementation requires a balance between global frameworks and local adaptation. Contextual sensitivity is crucial to ensure the framework not only meets global standards but also respects local languages, cultures, and educational traditions. Tailored strategies for each country's sociocultural and educational environment make DIGICOMPASS a flexible framework that harmonizes global goals with local needs.

Section 5.3 further highlights this adaptability, showing how DIGICOMPASS's phased integration approach allows for gradual implementation, continuous feedback, and refinement based on local contexts. This ensures the framework remains relevant and responsive, adapting to the unique needs and priorities of diverse educational settings. While DIGICOMPASS provides a robust structure for integrating global language education and digital literacy, it does not prescribe specific adaptations for every local context. Instead, it serves as a flexible guide that educators and policymakers can customize to suit their particular needs, supporting educational innovation while respecting the diversity of global education.

To enhance its comprehensive adoption and relevance, DIGICOMPASS aligns with key supranational frameworks such as the International Baccalaureate (IB), the UN SDGs, and the CEFR. These alignments ensure that DIGICOMPASS upholds rigorous academic standards, promotes intercultural understanding, and fosters global engagement. By doing so, DIGICOMPASS prepares students not only for academic success but also to be globally competent and socially responsible individuals, capable of contributing positively to an interconnected world.

Incorporating the UN SDGs into the DIGICOMPASS framework encourages students to think critically about global issues and empowers them to become agents of change. By embedding goals such as quality education, reduced inequalities, and peace, DIGICOMPASS fosters a sense of responsibility and ethical awareness. The CEFR's action-oriented approach to language education complements DIGICOMPASS's goals by emphasizing the co-construction of meaning through interaction. By integrating CEFR's proficiency scales and descriptors, DIGICOMPASS ensures comprehensive language education, including listening, speaking, reading, writing, and signing competencies. This alignment promotes plurilingual and pluricultural competence, sociolinguistic competence, and pragmatic competence, all essential components of intercultural competence, a key pillar of DIGICOMPASS. These alignments are the first step in integrating DIGICOMPASS into various educational systems, setting a strong foundation for future expansions. By aligning with national standards and international frameworks, DIGICOMPASS ensures that students are prepared to navigate and engage with a diverse, globalized world.

5.2.1 *National Education Standards and DIGICOMPASS Alignment*

DIGICOMPASS is designed to align with national educational standards, enhancing curriculum requirements and examination preparation across various countries:

- **AUSTRALIA**: Could be integrated into the general capabilities, such as digital literacy and intercultural understanding, and cross-curriculum Priorities that emphasize cultural diversity and ethical engagement. (Australian Curriculum, Assessment and Reporting Authority, 2022).
- **CANADA**: Can be customized to meet provincial needs, incorporating digital storytelling and supporting global competencies, aligning with provincial exams (Council of Ministers of Education, Canada, 2020).
- **ENGLAND**: Could enhance GCSEs and A Levels with digital literacy and global awareness, supporting interdisciplinary learning (Department for Education, England UK, 2014).
- **GHANA**: May be integrated into Social Studies, ICT, and Integrated Science, providing a broader global perspective and digital skills (Ministry of Education, Republic of Ghana, 2018).
- **INDIA**: Could align with the National Education Policy (NEP) 2020, enhancing digital literacy and global competencies in subjects like Social Studies, English, and Computer Science (Ministry of Education, Government of India, 2020).
- **IRELAND**: Has the potential to enhance Social, Personal, and Health Education (SPHE), Computer Science, and Geography, supporting portfolio and research components of exams (National Council for Curriculum and Assessment, Ireland, 2024).
- **KENYA**: Could reinforce the CBC's focus on competencies, integrating global citizenship, interdisciplinary learning and digital fluency into various subjects (Kenya Institute of Curriculum Development, 2019).
- **NEW ZEALAND**: May be woven into key competencies, engaging with global issues through digital platforms (New Zealand Ministry of Education, 2020).
- **SINGAPORE**: Supports subjects like English, Humanities, and CCE with projects that could enhance digital literacy and cross-cultural understanding (Ministry of Education, Singapore, 2020).
- **SOUTH AFRICA**: Has the potential to add value to Life Orientation, Social Sciences, and IT, promoting global citizenship and aiding NSC preparation (Department of Basic Education, Republic of South Africa, 2023).

(continued)

(continued)
- THE PHILIPPINES: Can align with holistic development goals, enriching subjects with global perspectives and digital competencies (Department of Education, Republic of the Philippines, 2019).
- UNITED STATES: Designed to be incorporated into English Language Arts and Social Studies, fostering interdisciplinary projects and offering preparatory content for AP courses (Common Core State Standards Initiative, 2021).

5.2.2 IB Curriculum and DIGICOMPASS Alignment

DIGICOMPASS's adaptability extends to international curricula like the IB program (International Baccalaureate Organization, 2025a, 2025b). Both DIGICOMPASS and the IB share a commitment to developing globally competent, well-rounded individuals equipped with critical thinking skills and intercultural understanding. However, several key differences distinguish DIGICOMPASS from the IB, each tailored to meet specific educational needs and contexts.

DIGICOMPASS weaves digital literacy into its curriculum more intensively than the IB, aiming to prepare students not just to use digital tools but to master them in ways that enhance communication, problem-solving, and global engagement. While project-based learning is an essential element of the IB, DIGICOMPASS embeds real-world projects more frequently and centrally. These projects tackle global challenges like climate change and social justice, integrating experiential learning to develop pragmatic problem-solving skills immediately applicable outside the classroom.

DIGICOMPASS is characterized by its adaptability to diverse educational standards and environments, offering significant flexibility to align with local and national educational needs. This is particularly valuable in multicultural and varied educational contexts where digital tools and resources need to be tailored to meet specific learner and community

Table 5.1 DIGICOMPASS mapping with IB curriculum: Year 7 to Year 12 progression

Year group	IB program	DIGICOMPASS integration	Activities
Years 7–8	MYP Years 1–2	Basic digital literacy, global awareness, cultural appreciation	Digital storytelling, virtual cultural exchanges, local-global projects
Years 9–10	MYP Years 3–4	Intermediate digital skills, global issue analysis, language skills	App/website development, digital simulations, international collaborations
Years 11–12	MYP Year 5, DP Year 1	Advanced digital literacy, extended essays, global model simulations	Hackathons, digital research for extended essay, intercultural negotiations

needs. DIGICOMPASS emphasizes the development of advanced pedagogical strategies incorporating cutting-edge educational technologies, including training teachers to use digital tools effectively and adapt teaching methods to enhance learning outcomes.

Additionally, DIGICOMPASS promotes the use of innovative digital assessment techniques, offering continuous and real-time feedback through technology-driven formative and summative tools. While the IB integrates digital tools selectively within its pedagogy, DIGICOMPASS systematically embeds advanced digital skills and literacy projects across subjects, ensuring their consistent application and real-world relevance at every educational stage. Furthermore, DIGICOMPASS enriches the IB's emphasis on international mindedness by intertwining global citizenship and intercultural competence into these digital projects. Table 5.1 provides an overview of the DIGICOMPASS-IB mapping by year group.

5.2.3 United Nations Sustainable Development Goals and DIGICOMPASS Alignment

The DIGICOMPASS framework is intrinsically aligned with the UN SDGs (United Nations, 2015), reflecting a shared commitment to fostering global citizenship (Table 5.2). At its core, DIGICOMPASS emphasizes global citizenship, integrating digital literacy, inclusive practices, intercultural competence, and awareness of social strategies to create a holistic and impactful educational experience.

Table 5.2 UN SDGs and DIGICOMPASS alignment

SDG	DIGICOMPASS	(Multi) literacies	Skills/competencies/ abilities	Activities
SDG 4: quality education	Digital literacy	Digital literacy, critical literacy, ethical literacy	Critical thinking, technical skills, ethical use of information	Global issue digital campaign
	Inclusive practices	Social literacy, cultural literacy, media literacy	Collaboration, empathy, accessibility	Collaborative digital storytelling
	Intercultural competence and plurilingualism	Intercultural literacy, plurilingual literacy	Cross-cultural communication, language proficiency, cultural awareness	Virtual cultural exchange
	Awareness of social strategies	Social literacy, ethical literacy	Ethical decision-making, social responsibility, critical reflection	Community service learning
SDG 10: reduced inequalities	Inclusive practices	Social literacy, cultural literacy, ethical literacy	Empathy, accessibility, equity	Community inclusion projects
	Awareness of social strategies	Ethical literacy, critical literacy	Ethical decision-making, social responsibility, critical reflection	Ethical dilemma simulation
SDG 11: sustainable cities and communities	Digital literacy	Digital literacy, innovation literacy	Urban planning, Digital mapping, innovation	Smart city projects
	Awareness of social strategies	Ethical literacy, social literacy	Community engagement, ethical planning	Urban ethics workshops
SDG 16: peace, justice, and strong institutions	Intercultural competence and plurilingualism	Intercultural literacy, plurilingual literacy	Mediation skills, conflict resolution, cross-cultural communication	Peacebuilding projects
	Awareness of social strategies	Ethical literacy, social literacy	Ethical governance, justice, social responsibility	Justice simulations

In pursuit of **quality education (SDG 4)**, DIGICOMPASS focuses on developing critical thinking, technical skills, and ethical use of information through digital literacy initiatives, such as global issue digital campaigns. Inclusive practices are emphasized to foster collaboration, empathy, and accessibility, as seen in collaborative digital storytelling projects. Intercultural competence is promoted through virtual cultural exchanges, enhancing cross-cultural communication and cultural awareness, while service-learning activities support ethical decision-making and social responsibility.

Addressing **reduced inequalities (SDG 10)**, the framework promotes empathy, accessibility, and equity through community inclusion projects and ethical dilemma simulations. These initiatives help students develop ethical decision-making skills and social responsibility, contributing to efforts to reduce inequalities in society.

To support **sustainable cities and communities (SDG 11)**, DIGICOMPASS integrates urban planning, digital mapping, and innovation into its curriculum. Through smart city projects, students apply these skills in real-world contexts, while urban ethics workshops engage them in community planning and ethical decision-making, ensuring sustainable development.

Finally, the framework's commitment to **peace, justice, and strong institutions (SDG 16)** is evident in activities that develop mediation skills, conflict resolution, and cross-cultural communication, such as peacebuilding projects. Justice simulations further enhance students' understanding of ethical governance, justice, and social responsibility, preparing them to contribute to peaceful and just societies.

Overall, DIGICOMPASS, grounded in constructivism, sociocultural theory, connectivism, and cognitive load theory, creates an inclusive learning environment. By fostering global citizenship through its core pillars, it equips students with the skills and knowledge necessary to contribute to a sustainable and equitable global society.

5.2.4 CEFR and DIGICOMPASS Alignment

CEFR (Council of Europe, 2001, 2020) is an established guideline used to measure and describe language proficiency across Europe and increasingly worldwide. It provides a standardized method for assessing and teaching languages, outlining clear proficiency scales ranging from Pre-A1 (beginner) to C2 (mastery). These scales are essential in aligning educational objectives with learners' capabilities and are used to gauge progress in language acquisition.

Central to the CEFR is its action-oriented approach, which positions learners as "social agents" who use language to perform specific tasks in real-life contexts. This approach emphasizes the practical application of language skills, focusing not just on isolated abilities but on the ability to use language effectively in diverse situations. Traditional language skills such as listening, speaking, reading, and writing are integrated within interaction and mediation activities. These activities require learners to mobilize their language skills dynamically, facilitating meaningful communication and comprehension in various contexts.

Plurilingualism, a key concept in the CEFR, values the linguistic and cultural diversity of learners. It encourages them to draw on their entire linguistic repertoire, promoting flexibility and adaptability in language use. The plurilingual vision emphasizes that languages and cultures are not compartmentalized but interact and contribute to a person's overall communicative competence. This approach aligns with DIGICOMPASS's goal of developing a comprehensive linguistic repertoire, preparing students to navigate multiple linguistic and cultural contexts effectively.

The CEFR includes interaction activities and mediation activities, both of which integrate traditional language skills. Interaction activities involve direct communication with others, requiring learners to listen, speak, read, and write interactively. Mediation activities, on the other hand, involve facilitating understanding and communication between speakers of different languages. These activities include tasks like translating, interpreting, summarizing, and explaining cultural references. By incorporating signing competences, the CEFR ensures inclusivity, enabling communication for deaf and hard-of-hearing individuals and aligning with DIGICOMPASS's commitment to inclusive practices.

Plurilingual and pluricultural competence is essential for developing intercultural competence, a pillar of the DIGICOMPASS curriculum. This competence involves using one's entire linguistic and cultural repertoire to communicate effectively, promoting both language learning and cultural awareness. Sociolinguistic competence, which includes understanding and using language appropriately in social contexts, and pragmatic competence, which involves organizing discourse and managing interactions, are both critical for navigating the complexities of intercultural communication.

Signing competence further enriches this framework, ensuring that learners can engage in multimodal communication. The integration of signing competence highlights the importance of inclusive practices, allowing for effective communication across different modalities and promoting a more comprehensive approach to language education.

In summary, the CEFR''s descriptors for interaction activities, mediation activities, plurilingual and pluricultural competence, sociolinguistic competence, pragmatic competence, and signing competence all contribute to developing intercultural competence. This integration aligns perfectly with the DIGICOMPASS curriculum, which aims to prepare students for active participation in a globalized world by fostering multilingual and intercultural literacy. Through this comprehensive approach, students not only achieve language proficiency but also gain the cultural and communicative skills necessary for global citizenship.

Table 5.3 aligns CEFR descriptors with DIGICOMPASS (multi)literacies, illustrating how various competencies are essential for developing intercultural competence.

5.3 Strategic Implementation

The modular, interdisciplinary design of DIGICOMPASS allows for gradual integration into various educational settings, aligning well with existing academic frameworks and specific institutional needs. By emphasizing core competencies such as digital literacy, global citizenship, and intercultural competence, DIGICOMPASS enhances student engagement through practical applications and cross-curricular projects. However,

Table 5.3 CEFR and DIGICOMPASS alignment

CEFR category	CEFR descriptors	CEFR level	(Multi)literacies
Interaction activities	Can initiate, maintain, and close simple face-to-face conversations on familiar topics	A2–B1	Enhances interactive and dialogic skills necessary for digital and face-to-face communication (oral, intercultural, social)
	Can use simple techniques to start, maintain, or end a conversation	A2–B1	Develops communication skills for diverse cultural interactions (oral, intercultural)

(*continued*)

Table 5.3 (continued)

CEFR category	CEFR descriptors	CEFR level	(Multi)literacies
Mediation activities	Facilitating collaborative interaction with peers: Can encourage others to contribute and ask questions to clarify understanding	B1–B2	Cultivates collaborative literacies through digital platforms and social media (collaborative, digital, intercultural)
	Collaborating to construct meaning: Can help to build a shared understanding by restating, rephrasing, and expanding on ideas	B2–C1	Develops critical thinking and collective knowledge-building skills (critical thinking, collaborative, digital)
	Managing interaction: Can manage interaction and participation to ensure the inclusion of all participants	B2–C1	Fosters inclusive communication strategies in diverse group settings (social, intercultural, leadership)
	Encouraging conceptual talk: Can encourage the exchange of ideas and viewpoints, fostering a deeper understanding of different perspectives	B2–C1	Promotes academic literacies by encouraging deep discussions on complex topics (critical thinking, intercultural, academic)
	Facilitating pluricultural space: Can facilitate the development of a space where cultural differences are acknowledged and respected	B2–C1	Encourages the creation of inclusive digital and physical spaces for intercultural dialogue (digital, intercultural, social)
	Acting as intermediary in informal situations: Can relay information from one person to another in informal settings	B1–B2	Develops informal communication and mediation skills essential for everyday intercultural interactions (interpersonal, intercultural)
	Facilitating communication in delicate situations and disagreements: Can mediate in sensitive contexts, ensuring respectful and constructive communication	B2–C1	Equips students with conflict resolution skills and cultural empathy (conflict resolution, interpersonal, intercultural)

(continued)

Table 5.3 (continued)

CEFR category	CEFR descriptors	CEFR level	(Multi)literacies
Plurilingual and pluricultural competence	Can use knowledge of contrasting genre conventions and textual patterns to support comprehension across languages	B1–B2	Develops genre awareness and multilingual comprehension strategies (multilingual, genre awareness, critical thinking)
	Can use their knowledge of various languages to aid comprehension in other languages	B1–B2	Enhances linguistic flexibility and adaptability in diverse communicative contexts (plurilingual, intercultural)
	Can recognize and apply cultural conventions in everyday social exchanges	A2–B1	Promotes intercultural pragmatics and social etiquette understanding (intercultural, social, pragmatic)
	Can show sensitivity to different cultures and recognize and respond to cultural cues in communication	A2–B1	Enhances intercultural awareness and sensitivity (intercultural, social, emotional)
	Can recognize and respond appropriately to social norms and conventions in different cultures	A1–A2	Builds foundational social and cultural literacy (social, cultural, intercultural)
	Can use simple words/signs and phrases from different languages to conduct a simple, practical transaction or information exchange	A1–A2	Develops basic plurilingual and intercultural communication skills (plurilingual, intercultural)

(continued)

Table 5.3 (continued)

CEFR category	CEFR descriptors	CEFR level	(Multi)literacies
Sociolinguistic competence	Can understand and apply sociolinguistic norms, such as levels of formality, politeness, and register	B1–B2	Develops social literacy skills, adapting language use to different social contexts and norms (social, pragmatic, interpersonal)
	Can adjust language use according to the context, audience, and purpose	B1–B2	Trains students in audience awareness and context-sensitive communication (contextual, social, interpersonal)
	Can act appropriately in everyday greetings, farewells, and expressions of thanks and apology, although they have difficulty coping with any departure from the routine	A2	Develops basic sociolinguistic competence in familiar social interactions (social, pragmatic, interpersonal)
Pragmatic competence	Can organize discourse effectively, using appropriate structures and cohesive devices	B1–B2	Promotes coherence and cohesion in both spoken and written communication (organizational, written, oral)
	Can use language functions appropriately to achieve specific communicative goals, such as requesting, apologizing, or giving advice	B1–B2	Enhances functional literacy by using language purposefully in various contexts (functional, contextual, interpersonal)
	Can recognize and produce fixed expressions and routines in everyday contexts	A1–A2	Builds foundational pragmatic skills for routine interactions (pragmatic, functional, social)
	Can participate in simple, direct conversations on familiar topics, with support if necessary	Pre-A1–A1	Develops initial interactive and pragmatic skills for basic communication (interactive, pragmatic, social)

(*continued*)

Table 5.3 (continued)

CEFR category	CEFR descriptors	CEFR level	(Multi)literacies
Signing competence	Can understand and use sign language structures and conventions appropriately	B1–B2	Develops inclusivity by incorporating sign language into communication activities (plurilingual, visual, gestural)
	Can mediate between spoken/written language and sign language, ensuring effective communication between deaf and hearing individuals	B2–C1	Promotes multimodal literacy by combining visual, gestural, and verbal communication forms (plurilingual, multimodal, intercultural)

effective implementation goes beyond mere alignment with academic standards; it requires a deep sensitivity to local contexts and the ability to adapt to diverse educational environments.

A successful implementation of DIGICOMPASS begins with a thorough needs assessment to identify curriculum gaps and understand the specific cultural, linguistic, and technological needs of the community. Gathering feedback from teachers, students, and administrators ensures that DIGICOMPASS aligns with existing standards and objectives while also tailoring the framework to respect local traditions, languages, and values. This recognition of local contexts is crucial, as it guides the customization of DIGICOMPASS modules to support both global and local educational goals.

Despite its adaptability, implementing DIGICOMPASS across different regions presents challenges, including varying levels of access to technology, cultural resistance to new educational practices, and differing educational policies. In areas where technological infrastructure is limited, such as rural communities, adopting offline resources or low-tech alternatives may be necessary to ensure all students benefit from the curriculum. Addressing cultural resistance requires proactive engagement with local communities through awareness campaigns and stakeholder meetings to build trust and foster acceptance of the DIGICOMPASS approach.

Following the needs assessment, the next step involves mapping the existing curriculum to align DIGICOMPASS modules with current standards, while also incorporating local priorities such as language and culturally relevant content. Collaboration with local educators and community leaders is essential to effectively tailor the framework, enhancing local educational goals without imposing a one-size-fits-all solution.

To manage implementation effectively, the DIGICOMPASS framework adopts a phased integration approach. This begins by introducing a few complementary modules, allowing for close monitoring and adjustments based on feedback and outcomes. This phased approach not only eases the integration process but also provides the flexibility to refine strategies to better suit local contexts. Regular feedback loops involving educators, students, and community members are critical for identifying areas that may require adaptation, ensuring that the DIGICOMPASS framework remains relevant and responsive.

Throughout the implementation process, maintaining cultural sensitivity and inclusivity is vital. Educators should receive training not only in digital tools and interdisciplinary teaching methods but also in cultural awareness, enabling them to respect and incorporate the diverse backgrounds of their students. This commitment to cultural sensitivity ensures that global citizenship education is delivered alongside an appreciation for local customs and values, fostering an inclusive learning environment where all students feel valued and understood.

By embedding these considerations into the strategic implementation process, DIGICOMPASS provides a robust and adaptable framework that supports global competencies while honoring the distinctiveness of local contexts. This approach ensures that the curriculum aligns with global standards while remaining relevant and meaningful to the communities it serves, ultimately enhancing the effectiveness and inclusivity of language education.

Table 5.4 outlines the phased approach for implementing and scaling DIGICOMPASS, detailing activities from initial planning and preparation to full-scale implementation. This structured timeline ensures meticulous planning, continuous improvement, and scalability. By following this strategic roadmap, schools can effectively integrate DIGICOMPASS, foster an inclusive and dynamic learning environment, and prepare students for success in a digital and interconnected world.

The long-term sustainability of the DIGICOMPASS curriculum relies heavily on continuous funding and resource allocation. Securing ongoing financial support ensures that the program can expand and evolve to meet the needs of all students. Several strategies are critical in achieving this goal.

Table 5.4 DIGICOMPASS strategic implementation and scalability

Phase	Month	Activities	Details	Outcomes
Phase 1: planning and preparation	1	Initial planning and needs assessment	Conduct meetings with administrators to outline the plan and set goals. Form implementation committee. Conduct needs assessment through surveys and focus groups. Analyze current curriculum to identify gaps	Goals set. Implementation committee formed. Curriculum gaps identified
		Develop curriculum map	Develop curriculum map aligning DIGICOMPASS with existing subjects. Create initial integration plan for Grade 9	Curriculum map developed. Initial integration plan created
	2	Professional development preparation	Plan and schedule initial training workshops. Prepare digital and offline resources for training	Training workshops scheduled. Resources prepared
		Develop training materials	Develop training materials focusing on core competencies and modular design	Training materials developed
	3	Resource development and community engagement	Create digital resources, lesson plans, multimedia content, and interactive activities. Customize resources to reflect local contexts. Provide offline resources for limited Internet access	Digital resources created. Resources customized. Offline resources available
		Engage community	Engage parents, community members, and local organizations through informational meetings. Establish feedback channels	Community engagement initiated. Feedback channels established

(continued)

Table 5.4 (continued)

Phase	Month	Activities	Details	Outcomes
Phase 2: initial implementation	4	Initial training and curriculum integration	Conduct week-long initial training workshop for Grade 9 teachers. Introduce DIGICOMPASS competencies and design	Teachers trained. DIGICOMPASS competencies introduced
		Begin integration	Begin integrating DIGICOMPASS modules into Grade 9 social studies and science courses. Provide ongoing support through peer mentoring and planning sessions	Integration started. Ongoing support provided
	5	Pilot program and continuous support	Launch pilot program in Grade 9. Facilitate bi-weekly planning sessions for interdisciplinary collaboration	Pilot program launched. Interdisciplinary collaboration initiated
		Monitor progress	Monitor progress and collect feedback from teachers and students. Provide continuous support through webinars and mentoring	Progress monitored. Continuous support provided
Phase 3: execution and feedback collection	6	Evaluation and adjustment	Conduct formative assessments to monitor student progress. Hold mid-term review meeting with implementation committee	Student progress assessed. Mid-term review conducted
		Adjust curriculum	Adjust curriculum integration and teaching strategies based on feedback. Plan additional training sessions as needed	Curriculum and strategies adjusted. Additional training planned

(*continued*)

Table 5.4 (continued)

Phase	Month	Activities	Details	Outcomes
Phase 4: expansion and scaling	7–9	Expansion to other grades	Evaluate success of pilot program. Develop plan for expanding integration to Grade 10	Pilot program evaluated. Expansion plan developed
		Begin integration	Begin gradual integration into Grade 10 courses. Continue professional development for new grades	Integration in Grade 10 started. Ongoing professional development
	10–12	Continuous improvement and scalability	Implement structured co-teaching models. Allocate regular planning time for co-teachers	Co-teaching models implemented. Planning time allocated
		Refine curriculum	Engage in iterative refinement of the curriculum. Involve community and stakeholders in review	Curriculum refined. Community review initiated
		Showcase projects	Showcase student projects to demonstrate impact	Student projects showcased
Phase 5: review and future planning	12	Comprehensive review	Conduct comprehensive review of the first year of implementation. Gather detailed feedback from all stakeholders	Implementation reviewed. Feedback gathered
		Future scalability plan	Develop plan for further scalability across all grades and regions	

Securing government grants and funding initiatives is essential for ongoing support from education departments and initiatives aimed at improving digital literacy and educational equity. Regular applications for grants focusing on technology integration and curriculum innovation can provide substantial financial resources. Additionally, establishing partnerships with private companies, particularly those in the technology sector, can provide additional financial support and resources. Companies might sponsor digital tools and devices or fund professional development programs, ensuring educators have access to the latest technologies.

Collaborating with educational foundations that support innovative educational practices can also be beneficial. These foundations often offer grants specifically for curriculum development and teacher training, providing a steady stream of funding. Utilizing crowdfunding platforms such as GoFundMe or DonorsChoose allows for fundraising for specific projects or resources. This strategy not only raises funds but also engages the broader community in supporting the curriculum. Developing programs to engage alumni can encourage contributions that help sustain and expand the curriculum. Alumni who have benefited from similar educational programs are often more inclined to support current students, ensuring a continuous flow of resources.

By implementing these strategies, the DIGICOMPASS curriculum can maintain its momentum, ensuring that it continues to provide high-quality, relevant education to all students. This comprehensive approach to funding and resource allocation is crucial for the long-term success and scalability of the program.

5.3.1 *Professional Development and Resource Development*

DIGICOMPASS is an interdisciplinary, modular framework specifically designed for secondary education. Its holistic approach integrates AI and XR technologies to personalize learning, incorporates inclusive practices to cater to diverse student needs, and utilizes experiential learning pedagogical approaches to deepen student engagement. Chapter 6 will illustrate how these elements come together to create a holistic and dynamic learning environment.

Professional development (PD) within the DIGICOMPASS framework goes beyond traditional training; it aims to empower secondary educators as active designers and implementers of this innovative curriculum. Initial workshops introduce educators to the core competencies and modular design of DIGICOMPASS, equipping them with the skills and confidence to effectively integrate AI, XR, inclusive practices, and experiential learning into their teaching. These workshops are designed to align with best practices in PD, emphasizing active learning, coherence with school goals, and a strong content focus, as recommended by Desimone and Garet (2015). Such workshops encourage creative thinking and foster a sense of ownership over the content educators deliver, promoting agency and innovation in their pedagogical practices.

Ongoing support is critical for the successful implementation of DIGICOMPASS. This support includes regular webinars, peer mentoring, and collaborative planning meetings, providing educators with continuous access to the latest educational strategies and digital tools. This sustained support is essential for fostering a culture of continuous professional growth, which aligns with Desimone and Garet's (2015) emphasis on the importance of PD that is ongoing, coherent, and sustained over time. By continuously engaging educators in professional learning communities (PLCs), DIGICOMPASS facilitates collective participation and the sharing of expertise across disciplines, which Desimone and Garet (2015) identify as key components of effective PD. PLCs encourage the development of interdisciplinary projects and collaborative problem-solving, ensuring that professional development is not a one-time event but an ongoing process of growth and adaptation.

Teacher-led classroom research, research mentorship, and PLCs are particularly well-suited for the DIGICOMPASS framework. Engaging in teacher-led research allows educators to explore and refine their practices within the DIGICOMPASS context, adapting strategies to meet the specific needs of their students and school environments. This process promotes reflective practice, critical thinking, and a deeper understanding of how to implement the curriculum's holistic approach effectively. Research mentorship, which involves experienced educators or researchers guiding teachers through the research process, enhances the quality and impact of teacher-led research by providing structured feedback and expert insights (Kemmis et al., 2014). This mentorship ensures that teacher-led research is rigorous, relevant, and aligned with the goals of DIGICOMPASS. PLCs provide a platform for educators to share their research findings, discuss challenges, and collaboratively develop solutions, fostering a shared sense of purpose and commitment to continuous improvement. Such ongoing professional development through teacher research, research mentorship, and PLCs significantly enhances teaching practices and improves student outcomes, as shown in studies by Desimone and Garet (2015) and Vescio et al. (2008).

The structured co-teaching model is another key component of professional development in DIGICOMPASS. By leveraging the strengths of multiple educators, co-teaching enhances curriculum delivery and creates dynamic, engaging learning environments. Models such as team teaching, parallel teaching, station teaching, alternative teaching, and the one teach, one assist approach allow for personalized instruction and targeted support, ensuring that all students benefit from the diverse expertise of their educators.

Design thinking workshops further enhance teaching practices by guiding educators through the process of creating engaging, relevant modules that bridge subjects such as digital technologies, languages, and social studies. These workshops involve a collaborative, iterative process that includes empathizing with student needs, defining educational challenges, ideating creative solutions, prototyping instructional strategies, and testing and refining these strategies. By engaging in design thinking, educators learn to develop innovative lesson plans and projects that resonate with students' interests and real-world applications.

Technology integration is crucial for the effective implementation of DIGICOMPASS. Educators need proficiency in advanced digital tools, including adaptive learning platforms for personalized instruction, collaborative tools for teamwork, immersive technologies like VR, AR, and MR for engaging learning experiences, and assistive technologies such as screen readers and speech-to-text software to support diverse learning needs. Chapter 3 provides a comprehensive discussion of these technologies and their application within the DIGICOMPASS framework.

Resource development is also a key focus, ensuring that digital resources—such as lesson plans, multimedia content, and interactive activities—are tailored to reflect local contexts and cultural relevance. Making these resources available across various digital platforms, including smartphones, tablets, and computers, ensures accessibility for students in different regions, particularly those with limited access to other technologies. This approach maximizes engagement and inclusivity, ensuring that all students can benefit from DIGICOMPASS.

In summary, professional development and resource development within the DIGICOMPASS framework are essential for empowering educators and ensuring the successful implementation of the curriculum. By promoting teacher-led research, incorporating research mentorship, fostering professional learning communities, and providing ongoing support and training, DIGICOMPASS encourages sustained professional growth and innovation in teaching practices. This comprehensive approach not only enhances educators' abilities and confidence but also creates a dynamic, inclusive, and engaging educational environment that meets the needs of all students.

5.4 Assessment, Evaluation, and Feedback

The DIGICOMPASS framework adopts an integrated approach to evaluation and feedback, ensuring that educational goals are closely aligned with actual student learning outcomes. This strategy intertwines student assessments with curriculum evaluations, creating a comprehensive system that captures the dynamic relationship between teaching and learning.

Central to this approach is the use of mixed-methods assessments. By combining quantitative tools such as standardized tests with qualitative methods like portfolios and projects, educators gain a holistic view of student abilities. This method assesses both foundational knowledge and applied skills, providing a detailed picture of each student's learning journey. Studies show that mixed-methods assessments provide a more comprehensive evaluation of student performance and learning outcomes (Stiggins, 2017).

Technology plays a pivotal role in facilitating continuous assessment and real-time feedback. Digital portfolios allow students to compile and showcase their work over time, offering a comprehensive view of their progress and development. Online quizzes provide immediate insights into student understanding, enabling educators to address knowledge gaps promptly. Furthermore, data analytics utilize machine learning models to predict student performance, identify key trends, and inform necessary curriculum adjustments. By analyzing factors such as online learning activities, term assessment grades, and academic emotions, educators can detect patterns that highlight students' academic strengths and areas needing improvement, thus enabling timely and targeted curriculum modifications (Namoun & Alshanqiti, 2021).

Interactive tools such as virtual polling and online discussion forums engage students actively in the feedback process. These tools gather immediate feedback on teaching strategies and curriculum content, allowing educators to make real-time adjustments.

5.4.1 Feedback Loop Integration and Personalized, Adaptive Learning

The integration of student and curriculum assessments creates a robust feedback loop, crucial for personalizing learning paths. Table 5.5 outlines the steps involved in this process within the framework.

Table 5.5 Feedback loop and personalized learning in DIGICOMPASS

Step	Description	Example/tools	Outcome
Data collection	Digital portfolios: Students regularly upload their work, providing a comprehensive view of their progress	Online quizzes, interactive tools, virtual polling, and discussion forums	Immediate feedback on student understanding and performance
Data analysis	Performance tracking: Data analytics tools analyze quiz results, portfolio submissions, and interaction data to identify trends and patterns in student performance	Data analytics tools	Identifies trends and patterns in student performance
Real-time adjustments	Adaptive learning technologies use this data to adjust the difficulty and pace of learning materials, ensuring tailored instruction for each student	AI-driven adaptive learning platforms	Ensures each student receives instruction tailored to their needs
Personalized learning paths	Platforms like Khan Academy use AI to tailor educational content to individual student needs, adapting in real-time	Personalized learning technologies	Provides a personalized learning experience that adapts in real-time
Differentiated instruction	Teachers use assessment data to provide varied resources and activities that cater to different learning profiles	Visual aids, multimedia resources, additional challenges for advanced students	Ensures all students receive appropriate challenges and support
Feedback implementation	Educators regularly review assessment data during structured feedback sessions to discuss student progress, identify areas for improvement, and refine instructional strategies	Scheduled feedback sessions, curriculum adjustments based on feedback	Ensures the curriculum remains relevant and effective

By continuously collecting and analyzing assessment data, DIGICOMPASS ensures that each student's learning path is dynamic and responsive. This ongoing process of assessment and feedback not only personalizes the learning experience but also enhances student engagement and maximizes learning outcomes. Regularly scheduled feedback sessions play a critical role in maintaining the relevance and effectiveness of a DIGICOMPASS curriculum. These sessions provide structured opportunities for educators to review assessment data, discuss student progress, and identify areas for improvement. By incorporating data analytics, these sessions become even more powerful. Educators can leverage detailed performance metrics to understand which aspects of the curriculum are working well and which need refinement.

In Chap. 3, several technologies were highlighted for their role in supporting these evaluation processes. While technology is a key component of the DIGICOMPASS evaluation strategy, other assessment methods are equally important. Teacher-student interactions, formative assessments, and peer assessments play crucial roles in evaluating student progress and providing feedback. These methods, emphasized in Chappuis et al. (2020), advocate for integrating assessment into daily teaching practices, setting clear learning targets, and involving students actively in their learning process through self and peer assessments. Effective feedback and diverse assessment methods are highlighted as essential for identifying learning gaps and informing instructional adjustments, ultimately enhancing student learning outcomes. Topping (2018) further supports the value of peer assessment, indicating its significant impact on student learning by fostering critical thinking and reflective skills through structured feedback processes.

5.4.2 Assessing Curriculum Relevance, Coherence, and Impact

Assessing the curriculum's relevance, coherence, and impact on learning outcomes is just as important as assessing student learning. A variety of methods can be employed to achieve this, each providing valuable insights into different aspects of the curriculum's effectiveness and alignment with educational goals.

First, surveys and questionnaires distributed to students, teachers, and parents serve as essential tools for gathering feedback on the curriculum's relevance and coherence. These instruments solicit opinions on the applicability of the curriculum content, the clarity and organization of the modules, and overall satisfaction. The collected data provide quantitative insights into how well the curriculum meets the needs of its stakeholders (Fullan, 2015).

In addition to surveys, focus groups with educators and students offer qualitative data on the curriculum's strengths and weaknesses. These discussions facilitate deeper insights into specific issues, allowing participants to provide detailed feedback and suggestions for improvement. Focus groups help identify areas where the curriculum excels and where it may require refinement (Krueger & Casey, 2015). Furthermore, curriculum mapping is an integral process in aligning DIGICOMPASS modules with national standards and learning objectives. This ensures that the curriculum is coherent and meets established educational benchmarks. Regular reviews and updates of the curriculum map are essential to maintain alignment and address any gaps or redundancies (Jacobs, 2004).

To measure long-term impact, longitudinal studies track student progress over several years. By analyzing data on student achievements, graduation rates, and college enrollments, these studies provide a comprehensive assessment of the curriculum's effectiveness in preparing students for future academic and career success. Mertens (2024) emphasizes the importance of integrating diverse research methods and ethical considerations when conducting these evaluations, ensuring that the findings are robust and culturally responsive. Moreover, utilizing performance metrics through data analytics allows for the continuous assessment of the curriculum's impact on student learning outcomes.

Monitoring key performance indicators (KPIs) such as test scores, project completion rates, and engagement levels provides a clear picture of how well students are performing and engaging with the curriculum. These metrics highlight areas for potential improvement (Pellegrino & Hilton, 2012). Additionally, engaging external experts to conduct audits of the curriculum offers unbiased evaluations of its effectiveness and relevance. These audits involve a thorough review of the curriculum content, teaching methods, and assessment strategies, with a focus on integrating diverse research methods and ethical practices (Mertens, 2024). External auditors can offer recommendations for adjustments and enhancements, ensuring that the curriculum remains up-to-date and impactful (Guskey, 2000; OECD, 2019).

In summary, the assessment, evaluation, and feedback processes within DIGICOMPASS create a continuous cycle of improvement. Through a blend of mixed-methods assessments, real-time feedback facilitated by advanced technologies, and structured feedback loops, the curriculum remains dynamic and effective.

5.5 Strategic Solutions for Inclusive Education

To ensure that DIGICOMPASS is accessible and inclusive, various strategies can be employed to address diverse educational needs and contexts globally. Emphasizing digital literacy, flexibility, and adaptability are essential to reach all students effectively.

5.5.1 Enhancing Accessibility Through Technology

Ensuring that all students can access and benefit from a DIGICOMPASS curriculum involves addressing the technology challenges that contribute to the digital divide. This approach includes adopting user-friendly e-learning platforms, improving digital infrastructure, and offering comprehensive training programs to enhance digital literacy. Here's a breakdown of practical steps to achieve this:

Practical Steps

- *Device Compatibility:* Ensure that curriculum content is accessible on various devices, prioritizing smartphones due to their widespread use. This enables students to engage with learning materials on smartphones, tablets, and computers.
- *Content Formats:* Develop both digital and adaptable offline content formats to ensure that DIGICOMPASS remains accessible in areas with limited Internet connectivity. By offering downloadable resources, students can stay engaged even without continuous Internet access.
- *Infrastructure Investment:* Advocate for investments in digital infrastructure, especially in underserved areas, to improve Internet access. This can involve collaborating with government agencies and private companies to expand broadband coverage.
- *Partnerships:* Establish partnerships with technology companies, non-profits, and government agencies to facilitate access to necessary hardware and connectivity for students from underserved communities.

- *Training Programs*: Implement comprehensive training programs aimed at both students and educators to enhance digital literacy. These programs should focus on equipping participants with the skills needed to navigate digital platforms confidently.
- *Policy Advocacy:* Work with policymakers to develop and enforce regulations that promote equitable access to digital resources. This might include increasing technology funding for schools and extending broadband access to rural and underserved areas.
- *Assistive Technologies:* Employ assistive technologies, such as screen readers and speech-to-text programs, to support students with disabilities. This ensures that digital content is accessible to all students.
- *Culturally Sensitive Content:* Design digital content that is culturally relevant and available in multiple languages, addressing cultural and language differences that might otherwise pose barriers to engagement.
- *Community and Parental Involvement*: Emphasize the significant role of family and community in the educational process. This can include creating community portals that allow families to engage with and understand the educational technologies used, or hosting community tech days to involve the broader community in school tech initiatives.

Example

- In Kenya, the Digital Literacy Programme has provided devices to primary school students and trained teachers to integrate technology into their classrooms. This initiative, supported by partnerships with international tech companies, has significantly improved digital literacy and access to educational resources. The government has connected over one million digital learning devices to more than 20,000 public primary schools. The program also includes efforts to train teachers to effectively incorporate these devices into their teaching, fostering an engaging and modern learning environment (Wanjiru & Kibet, 2021).

5.5.2 *Multi-platform Availability and Multilingual Support*

DIGICOMPASS content is designed to be accessible across multiple platforms, including smartphones, tablets, and computers, ensuring students in various regions can engage with the curriculum. Given the widespread use of smartphones, particularly in areas with limited access to other technologies, this approach maximizes reach. Although offline resources, such as printed materials and downloadable content, are considered temporary measures, the ultimate goal is to transition all students to digital platforms. Digital literacy is a core pillar of the DIGICOMPASS framework. Additionally, acknowledging the linguistic diversity of Global Classrooms, DIGICOMPASS supports multiple languages through subtitles, translation options, and multilingual support materials, enhancing engagement and comprehension for non-native English speakers.

Practical Steps

- *Device Compatibility:* Ensure curriculum content is accessible on various devices, prioritizing smartphones due to their widespread use.
- *Content Formats:* Develop both digital and offline content formats, providing downloadable resources for areas with limited Internet access.
- *Language Support:* Implement multilingual support, including subtitles and translations, to cater to diverse linguistic needs.
- *User Testing:* Conduct usability testing across different platforms to ensure a seamless user experience for all students.

Example

- In India, the use of smartphones for educational content has been widely adopted due to their accessibility and affordability. The Indian government's "DIKSHA" platform provides digital resources in multiple languages, ensuring broader reach and comprehension. The platform offers a comprehensive repository of learning resources aligned with the curriculum for various grades and subjects. It supports 36 Indian languages, catering to diverse educational needs and promoting inclusivity. DIKSHA also provides features such as QR codes for easy access to lessons, interactive material, practice exercises, and assessments for both teachers and students (Ministry of Education, Government of India, 2017).

5.5.3 Partnerships with Community Organizations and NGOs

Partnerships with community organizations and NGOs are vital for extending a DIGICOMPASS curriculum's reach, especially in diverse and underserved areas. These partnerships provide essential resources like learning materials and technology, key in regions with limited educational infrastructure, and offer venues for instructional sessions, broadening curriculum access. Leveraging their deep community ties, these organizations support educators in adapting and delivering a DIGICOMPASS curriculum in culturally relevant ways, integrating local languages and contexts to enhance student engagement and comprehension.

Practical Steps

- *Identify Key Stakeholders:* Map out potential community organizations and NGOs that align with DIGICOMPASS's educational goals.
- *Engagement Initiatives:* Host community meetings, workshops, and forums to introduce the DIGICOMPASS curriculum and its benefits.
- *Collaboration Agreements:* Formalize partnerships through Memorandums of Understanding (MOUs) to clearly define roles, responsibilities, and goals.
- *Joint Programs:* Develop collaborative programs where community organizations co-host educational events, provide guest speakers, or facilitate workshops.
- *Continuous Communication:* Maintain regular communication with partners through newsletters, progress reports, and feedback sessions to keep them engaged and informed.

Example

- In Poland, the EU-funded "Remote School" initiative has significantly enhanced educational resources and infrastructure, especially during the COVID-19 pandemic. Launched in 2020, the project provided over EUR 82 million to equip more than 23,000 schools with digital learning devices and resources, benefiting approximately 335,000 students. This initiative ensured that students could continue their education remotely, addressing the digital divide and enhancing access to quality education in remote and underserved areas (European Commission, 2020).

5.5.4 Addressing Financial Barriers

Understanding the financial barriers that may limit some students' participation in a DIGICOMPASS curriculum, there is hope to collaborate with local businesses, educational foundations, and government programs to explore potential scholarships and grants. The goal is to eventually provide students in need with access to tablets, the Internet, and other technological tools, helping to ensure that all learners have the opportunity to benefit from this innovative educational approach.

Practical Steps

- *Grant Writing Workshops:* Offer training sessions for educators on how to write effective grant proposals.
- *Local Business Engagement:* Create partnerships with local businesses to sponsor technology and resources for students.
- *Educational Foundations:* Apply for grants from educational foundations that support technology integration in schools.
- *Government Programs:* Leverage government funding initiatives aimed at improving digital literacy and educational equity.
- *Crowdfunding Campaigns:* Use platforms like GoFundMe or DonorsChoose to raise funds for specific projects or resources.

Example

- In the United States, the "ConnectED" initiative by the Obama administration secured commitments from private companies to provide over $2 billion in technology resources to schools, bridging the digital divide for many students. This initiative significantly improved access to high-speed Internet and educational technology in K-12 schools and libraries, enabling enhanced learning opportunities for students across the country (The White House, Office of the Press Secretary, 2015).

5.5.5 Professional Development and Professional Growth

Professional development (PD) within DIGICOMPASS is structured to empower teachers to become active designers and implementers of the curriculum. PD sessions focus on collaborative teaching strategies, encouraging educators from diverse disciplines to merge their expertise effectively. These workshops foster a cooperative environment where teachers learn to plan, teach, and assess together, extending beyond mere integration of teaching styles to include conflict resolution and joint decision-making. Additionally, ensuring all educators are proficient in using modern digital tools is crucial for effective curriculum delivery. This includes leveraging AI-driven platforms for real-time data tracking and adaptive learning, enhancing digital teaching methods, and improving student engagement and learning outcomes.

Practical Steps

- *Initial Workshops:* Conduct comprehensive workshops to familiarize educators with the DIGICOMPASS framework, focusing on its core competencies and modular design.
- *Ongoing Support:* Provide continuous PD opportunities through webinars, peer mentoring, and collaborative planning sessions.
- *Technology Proficiency:* Ensure educators are proficient in using modern digital tools, leveraging AI-driven platforms for real-time data tracking and adaptive learning.
- *Collaborative Strategies:* Promote collaborative teaching strategies, encouraging educators from different disciplines to merge their expertise effectively.
- *Feedback and Improvement:* Regularly collect feedback from teachers and use it to refine PD programs, ensuring they meet the evolving needs of educators.

Example

- In Singapore, the Ministry of Education's professional development programs include extensive training on using digital tools and collaborative teaching strategies. Teachers receive ongoing support through a structured mentorship system and professional learning communities. This support is part of a broader effort to enhance digital literacy and integrate technology into teaching practices, ensuring that educators can effectively use these tools to improve student outcomes (Ministry of Education, Singapore, 2021).

5.5.6 Enhancing Teacher Collaboration and Peer Learning

A key strategic solution for implementing DIGICOMPASS is fostering collaboration and peer learning among educators. This approach not only builds a supportive teaching community but also leverages the collective expertise of educators to enhance curriculum delivery and student outcomes. By encouraging teachers to share best practices, co-plan lessons, and engage in professional learning communities, DIGICOMPASS ensures that educators are continuously improving and adapting their methods to meet diverse student needs.

Practical Steps

- *Establish Interdisciplinary Professional Learning Communities (PLCs):* Create PLCs within schools where teachers from different subjects can regularly meet to discuss challenges, share strategies, and collaborate on lesson planning, particularly for the interdisciplinary and modular nature of DIGICOMPASS.
- *Schedule Collaborative Planning Time:* Allocate dedicated time during the school week for teachers to co-plan lessons and units, ensuring they have the opportunity to integrate various teaching approaches and perspectives.
- *Peer Observation and Feedback:* Encourage teachers to observe each other's classes and provide constructive feedback, fostering a culture of continuous improvement and mutual support.
- *Collaborative Resource Development:* Facilitate the creation and development of teaching resources collaboratively. This includes interdisciplinary lesson plans, multimedia content, and interactive activities that can be used across different subjects.
- *Online Collaboration Platforms:* Utilize digital platforms to facilitate ongoing collaboration and resource sharing among teachers, especially for those who may not have frequent in-person interaction.
- *Recognition Programs:* Implement programs that recognize and reward collaborative efforts and innovative teaching practices, motivating teachers to engage in peer learning and collaboration.

Example

- *Canada's Teacher Learning and Leadership Program (TLLP):* Canada's Ontario Ministry of Education runs the Teacher Learning and Leadership Program (TLLP), which emphasizes collaboration and peer learning among educators. The TLLP encourages teachers to work together on projects that enhance their professional practice and improve student outcomes. Through this program, teachers across various disciplines collaborate to develop innovative teaching methods and resources, share best practices, and receive funding to implement their projects. The program fosters a culture of continuous professional growth and collegial support, leading to improved educational practices and student learning experiences (Lieberman et al., 2016).

5.5.7 *Community and Stakeholder Engagement*

Involving parents, community members, and local organizations in the implementation process is crucial for building support and ensuring the curriculum meets community needs. Creating platforms for ongoing dialogue to gather feedback and incorporate insights from stakeholders strengthens community ties and increases investment in the curriculum.

Practical Steps

- *Parent-Teacher Conferences:* Organize regular parent-teacher conferences to discuss the curriculum and student progress and gather feedback from parents.
- *Advisory Boards:* Establish community advisory boards that meet quarterly to discuss curriculum implementation and outcomes.
- *Feedback Platforms:* Create online platforms for parents and community members to provide ongoing feedback and suggestions.
- *Outreach Programs:* Develop outreach programs to engage local organizations and stakeholders in supporting the curriculum.
- *Collaborative Events:* Host events that involve the community in curriculum-related activities, such as workshops, exhibitions, and cultural fairs.

Example

- The Australian Council for Educational Research (ACER) has documented how schools in Australia have successfully organized community fairs and exhibitions to showcase student projects. These events engage the wider community and help secure support for educational initiatives. Schools utilize these exhibitions to display student work, which not only celebrates student achievements but also fosters community involvement and support for educational programs (Earp, 2016).

DIGICOMPASS takes a multifaceted approach to promoting accessibility and inclusivity in education, rooted in both theoretical foundations and practical strategies. By addressing technology challenges, promoting device compatibility, and advancing culturally sensitive content, the framework seeks to collaborate with community organizations to expand equitable access to digital learning for all students, regardless of their background. The integration of assistive technologies, policy advocacy, and professional development further strengthens this inclusive vision. Through ongoing engagement with communities and stakeholders, DIGICOMPASS strives to foster an educational environment where every student can thrive, embodying the principles of global citizenship, empathy, and ethical digital engagement.

5.6 Conclusion

This chapter illustrates how DIGICOMPASS offers a versatile and adaptable framework for integrating global citizenship education. Its alignment with both national and supranational standards ensures the framework's applicability across diverse educational settings. By focusing on professional development, ongoing support, and the integration of advanced digital technologies, DIGICOMPASS enhances educators' ability to address diverse student needs. The phased implementation strategy supports sustainable integration and is bolstered by strategies for financial sustainability and community engagement. The chapter highlights the importance of inclusivity, accessibility, contextual sensitivity, and cultural relevance, ensuring that the DIGICOMPASS framework remains relevant, adaptable, and effective in promoting global competencies.

References

Australian Curriculum, Assessment and Reporting Authority. (2022). *Australian Curriculum* (Version 9.0). https://v9.australiancurriculum.edu.au/

Chappuis, J., Stiggins, R. J., Chappuis, S., & Arter, J. (2020). *Classroom assessment for student learning: Doing it right-using it well* (p. 432). Pearson.

Common Core State Standards Initiative. (2021). *Common core state standards.* https://www.thecorestandards.org/

Council of Europe. (2001). *Common European framework of reference for languages: Learning, teaching, assessment.* Cambridge University Press. https://rm.coe.int/1680459f97

Council of Europe. (2020). *Common European framework of reference for languages: Learning, teaching, assessment – Companion volume.* Council of Europe. https://rm.coe.int/common-european-framework-of-reference-for-languages-learning-teaching/16809ea0d4

Council of Ministers of Education, Canada. (2020). *Pan-Canadian systems-level framework on global competencies.* https://static1.squarespace.com/static/5af1e87f5cfd79c163407ead/t/5e20d79f9713f543996da6ad/1579210656022/Pan-Canadian+Systems-Level+Framework+on+Global+Competencies_EN.pdf

Department for Education, England UK. (2014). *National curriculum in England: Framework for key stages 1 to 4.* https://www.gov.uk/government/publications/national-curriculum-in-england-framework-for-key-stages-1-to-4/the-national-curriculum-in-england-framework-for-key-stages-1-to-4

Department of Basic Education, Republic of South Africa. (2023). *FET programmes of assessments 2023–2024.* https://www.education.gov.za/Portals/0/Documents/Publications/National%20Circulars/FET%20Programmes%20of%20Assessments%202023-2024.pdf?ver=2023-04-19-135036-113

Department of Education, Republic of the Philippines. (2019). *Policy guidelines on the K to 12 basic education program.* https://www.deped.gov.ph/wp-content/uploads/2019/08/DO_s2019_021.pdf

Desimone, L. M., & Garet, M. S. (2015). Best practices in teachers' professional development in the United States. *Psychology, Society & Education, 7*(3), 252–263. https://repositorio.ual.es/bitstream/handle/10835/3930/Desimone%20En%20ingles.pdf?se

Earp, J. (2016). School exhibitions – Tips to involve all your students. *Teacher Magazine, Australian Council for Educational Research.* https://www.teachermagazine.com/au_en/articles/school-exhibitions-tips-to-involve-all-your-students

European Commission. (2020). *Equipping students in Poland for remote learning during COVID-19.* https://ec.europa.eu/regional_policy/projects/projects-database/equipping-students-in-poland-for-remote-learning-during-covid-19_en

Fullan, M. (2015). *The new meaning of educational change* (5th ed.). Teachers College Press.

Guskey, T. R. (2000). *Evaluating professional development.* Corwin Press.

International Baccalaureate Organization. (2025a). *MYP curriculum.* https://www.ibo.org/programmes/middle-years-programme/curriculum/

International Baccalaureate Organization. (2025b). *DP curriculum.* https://www.ibo.org/programmes/diploma-programme/curriculum/
Jacobs, H. H. (2004). *Getting results with curriculum mapping.* ASCD.
Kemmis, S., Wilkinson, J., Edwards-Groves, C., Hardy, I., Grootenboer, P., & Bristol, L. (2014). *Changing practices, changing education.* Springer.
Kenya Institute of Curriculum Development. (2019). *Basic Education Curriculum Framework.* https://kicd.ac.ke/curriculum-reform/basic-education-curriculum-framework/
Krueger, R. A., & Casey, M. A. (2015). *Focus groups: A practical guide for applied research* (5th ed.). SAGE Publications.
Lieberman, A., Campbell, C., & Yashkina, A. (2016). *Teacher learning and leadership: Of, by, and for teachers.* Routledge.
Mertens, D. M. (2024). *Research and evaluation in education and psychology: Integrating diversity with quantitative, qualitative, and mixed methods* (6th ed.). Sage Publications.
Ministry of Education, Government of India. (2017). *Digital Infrastructure for Knowledge Sharing (DIKSHA).* https://diksha.gov.in/
Ministry of Education, Government of India. (2020). *National education policy 2020.* https://www.education.gov.in/nep/about-nep
Ministry of Education, Republic of Ghana. (2018). *Ghana education reform.* https://moe.gov.gh/index.php/education-reform/
Ministry of Education, Singapore. (2020). *Learn for life – Ready for the future: Refreshing our curriculum and skillsfuture for educators.* https://www.moe.gov.sg/news/press-releases/20200304-learn-for-life-ready-for-the-future-refreshing-our-curriculum-and-skillsfuture-for-educators
Ministry of Education, Singapore. (2021). *Support for teachers.* https://www.moe.gov.sg/news/parliamentary-replies/20211101-support-for-teachers
Namoun, A., & Alshanqiti, A. (2021). Predicting student performance using data mining and learning analytics techniques: A systematic literature review. *Applied Sciences, 11*(1), 237. https://doi.org/10.3390/app11010237
National Council for Curriculum and Assessment, Ireland. (2024). *Curriculum online.* https://curriculumonline.ie/
New Zealand Ministry of Education. (2020). *Key competencies.* https://nzcurriculum.tki.org.nz/Key-competencies
OECD. (2019). *Future of education and skills 2030: Curriculum analysis.* https://one.oecd.org/document/EDU/EDPC(2019)16/en/pdf
Pellegrino, J. W., & Hilton, M. L. (Eds.). (2012). *Education for life and work: Developing transferable knowledge and skills in the 21st century.* National Academies Press.
Stiggins, R. J. (2017). *The perfect assessment system.* ASCD.

The White House, Office of the Press Secretary. (2015). *FACT SHEET: ConnectED: Two years of delivering opportunity to K-12 schools & libraries.* https://obamawhitehouse.archives.gov/the-press-office/2015/06/25/fact-sheet-connected-two-years-delivering-opportunity-k-12-schools

Topping, K. J. (2018). *Using peer assessment to inspire reflection and learning.* Routledge.

United Nations. (2015). *Transforming our world: The 2030 agenda for sustainable development.* https://sdgs.un.org/sites/default/files/publications/21252030%20Agenda%20for%20Sustainable%20Development%20web.pdf

Vescio, V., Ross, D., & Adams, A. (2008). A review of research on the impact of professional learning communities on teaching practice and student learning. *Teaching and Teacher Education, 24*(1), 80–91. https://doi.org/10.1016/j.tate.2007.01.004

Wanjiru, A., & Kibet, W. (2021). One million digital learning devices connected to schools. *Kenya News Agency.* https://www.kenyanews.go.ke/a-million-digital-learning-devices-connected-to-schools/

CHAPTER 6

AI-XR for Personalized and Experiential Learning in DIGICOMPASS

Abstract This chapter examines the integration of AI and extended reality (XR) technologies within the DIGICOMPASS framework to advance personalized and experiential learning. AI technologies provide real-time feedback, adaptive pathways, and personalized learning experiences, while XR creates immersive environments for engaging exploration of global challenges. Approaches like scenario-based learning, project-based learning, inquiry-based learning, and content and language integrated learning foster critical thinking, collaboration, and multilingual proficiency, supported by inclusive practices such as universal design for learning, culturally responsive education, and social-emotional learning to ensure accessibility, cultural responsiveness, and emotional support. The chapter highlights the synergy between adaptivity, differentiation, and experiential strategies, showcasing how these innovations enhance engagement and intercultural competence. A practical module on climate change education exemplifies AI and XR's transformative potential, emphasizing scientific inquiry, cultural awareness, and multilingual communication to prepare learners for success in diverse, digitally connected contexts.

Keywords AI-XR • Adaptivity • Differentiation • Experiential learning • Personalized learning

6.1 Introduction

The integration of advanced technologies such as AI and XR offers unprecedented opportunities to enhance both learning and teaching. This chapter explores their applications within the DIGICOMPASS framework, highlighting how these tools can redefine pedagogical approaches to create inclusive, engaging, and effective educational experiences. By focusing on specific strategies and practices, we emphasize the potential of AI and XR to cultivate twenty-first-century global citizens. At the end of the chapter, the practical module serves as a tangible example of how educators can seamlessly incorporate these innovations into their curricula, ensuring that technology enhances rather than complicates the educational process.

6.2 DIGICOMPASS Holistic Pedagogy

At the heart of this pedagogy lies **personalization**, the foundational core built on **adaptivity** and **differentiation** (Fig. 6.1). Adaptive learning utilizes technology and real-time feedback to dynamically adjust the learning experience, while differentiated instruction customizes teaching and assessment to cater to students' diverse abilities and needs. Personalized learning is the core because it ensures that every student's educational journey is uniquely tailored.

> Surrounding this core are **experiential learning** approaches, designed to translate personalized strategies into action by engaging students in active, real-world tasks and problem-solving:
>
> - **Project-Based Learning (PBL)**: Involves students in extended projects that they choose and develop, working at their own pace with differentiated support to solve real-world problems.
> - **Inquiry-Based Learning (IBL)**: Encourages students to explore questions that matter to them, with personalized guidance that supports their inquiry process and deepens their understanding.

(*continued*)

(continued)
- **Scenario-Based Learning (SBL)**: Places students in realistic scenarios that reflect their own life contexts or future goals, with adaptive elements that respond to their decisions and learning progress.
- **Content and Language Integrated Learning (CLIL)**: Combines content and language learning in a way that is personalized to each student's language proficiency and subject matter interest.

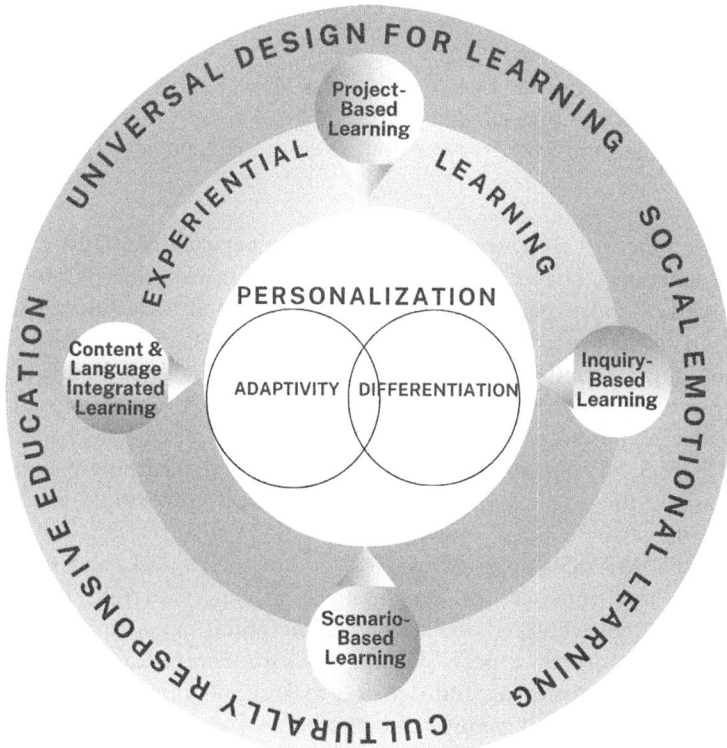

Fig. 6.1 Personalized and experiential learning in DIGICOMPASS

These approaches are further supported by inclusive practices that represent the "East" of DIGICOMPASS (see Chap. 2) and focus on accessibility, cultural relevance, and emotional well-being. Encircling the personalized and experiential approaches are three essential inclusive practices:

- **Universal Design for Learning (UDL)**: Ensures that all personalized learning strategies are accessible from the outset, accommodating the widest possible range of learners by reducing barriers to learning.
- **Culturally Responsive Education (CRE)**: Embeds students' cultural backgrounds into the learning process, making education more engaging and relevant by honoring and reflecting the diverse identities within the classroom.
- **Social-Emotional Learning (SEL)**: Develops each student's social and emotional skills through personalized strategies that recognize and support their unique emotional and social needs.

These practices are essential to a synergetic **personalized and experiential learning**. They ensure that the learning environment is not only personalized and experiential but also inclusive, culturally relevant, and emotionally supportive. Experiential learning, as conceptualized by Kolb (2015), aligns with the instructional design framework for authentic learning environments proposed by Herrington and Oliver (2000), serving as a practical embodiment of DIGICOMPASS's theoretical underpinnings (see Chap. 3). By placing experience at the core of the learning process, it emphasizes the cyclical process of experiencing, reflecting, thinking, and acting.

DIGICOMPASS's approaches—that is, SBL, PBL, IBL, and CLIL—exemplify the principles of experiential learning, fostering inclusivity through student-centered, collaborative methods that actively engage, value, and support all learners. SBL immerses students in realistic scenarios requiring problem-solving and decision-making, aligning with constructivist principles by engaging students in active learning. It reflects sociocultural theory by promoting social interactions and collaboration. Connectivism is evident as students use technology to simulate real-world contexts. By applying cognitive load theory, scenarios are designed to be manageable and enhance learning.

PBL involves students in real-world projects, fostering deep understanding through sustained inquiry and collaboration (Kokotsaki et al., 2016). It aligns with constructivism by allowing students to construct knowledge through meaningful projects. Sociocultural theory is reflected in the collaborative nature of PBL, where students work together and learn from each other. PBL supports connectivism by incorporating digital tools and resources, and cognitive load theory by structuring projects to avoid cognitive overload. IBL complements PBL by encouraging students to ask questions and seek answers through exploration and investigation, fostering deep understanding and critical thinking skills (Pedaste et al., 2015). It supports constructivism through active, student-driven inquiry and aligns with sociocultural theory by encouraging collaborative exploration and discussion. IBL incorporates connectivist principles by utilizing technology for research and inquiry and applies cognitive load theory by scaffolding the inquiry process to ensure it is manageable.

Both PBL and IBL are essential for engaging students in their learning process. Like SBL, PBL and IBL engage students collaboratively, and so does CLIL, where students learn a subject through the medium of another language. This dual-focused approach enhances both language proficiency and subject knowledge, supporting multilingualism and preparing students for global interactions (Coyle et al., 2010). CLIL effectively promotes language abilities alongside academic content, offering a holistic educational experience that integrates multiple sources and forms of knowledge (Nikula et al., 2016). This approach aligns with constructivism by engaging students in meaningful content learning through language. Sociocultural theory is reflected in the interactive, communicative nature of language learning. CLIL integrates connectivist principles by using technology to access diverse content and linguistic resources. Cognitive load theory is applied by carefully balancing language and content complexity to optimize learning.

Together, these approaches underscore the importance of a student-centered, inclusive, and experiential pedagogy, providing a rich educational environment that promotes critical thinking, collaboration, and cultural competence. As we move forward, the integration of AI and XR technologies presents new opportunities to further personalize learning experiences. These technologies enhance the adaptability and immersion of experiential learning, offering real-time feedback and tailored educational pathways. The following sections will explore how AI-XR can be leveraged to deepen personalized learning and experiential education within the DIGICOMPASS framework, enhancing both the effectiveness and engagement of students in diverse learning environments.

6.2.1 AI-XR Personalized Learning

Personalized learning is a pedagogy that tailors education to the unique needs, abilities, and modalities of each student. This approach recognizes the diversity in how learners absorb, process, and apply information, necessitating an adaptable educational strategy. By centering the learning process around the student, personalized learning ensures a more relevant, engaging, and effective educational experience (Pane et al., 2017).

Adaptivity is a vital component of personalized learning, driven by AI technologies. Adaptive learning systems use algorithms and real-time data to monitor student performance, identifying patterns, strengths, and challenges. These systems adjust the learning experience to meet specific needs, providing personalized feedback, modifying task difficulty, and recommending new learning materials (Froloviceva, 2022). Platforms like DreamBox and Knewton offer adaptive learning environments that dynamically modify the instructional path based on a student's responses. If a student struggles with a concept, the system provides additional resources and alternative explanations until mastery is achieved; if the student excels, more complex challenges are introduced to keep them engaged and progressing (Pane et al., 2017). At the Singapore International School, technology integration enhances personalized learning through adaptive strategies and differentiation. Teachers use data analytics to monitor progress and identify areas needing additional support, allowing real-time adjustments to the learning experience. This approach combines adaptivity and differentiation by using digital portfolios and data analytics to customize instruction according to each student's learning needs, fostering both academic performance and global citizenship (Lim-Ratnam, 2019).

XR further enhances adaptivity by creating immersive learning environments that dynamically respond to a student's actions and progress. In XR settings, such as Labster's VR simulations for scientific experiments, the environment adapts to the learner's input, adjusting the complexity of tasks based on progress and understanding. This ensures that all students, regardless of their starting point, can engage with the material in a way that is both challenging and accessible (Makransky & Mayer, 2022).

Differentiated instruction complements adaptivity by tailoring teaching approaches, content, and assessments to meet the diverse needs of learners within the same classroom. AI tools like ScribeSense facilitate this process by analyzing handwritten student work across various subjects, identifying learning gaps, and providing targeted feedback. For example, they can recommend additional practice problems in math, highlight structural issues in essays, or identify misconceptions in science lab reports. By automating repetitive tasks like grading and providing actionable insights, ScribeSense enables teachers to focus on creative lesson planning, personalized support, and fostering deeper engagement. Rather than replacing educators, such tools enhance their capacity to meet the unique needs of every student, making instruction more responsive and impactful.

XR technologies also support differentiation by offering varied experiences within the same learning scenario. For example, in a history class using XR, students might virtually walk through ancient civilizations, with the experience adjusting the complexity of information based on the student's prior knowledge and learning pace, ensuring that all students can engage with the material in a way that is challenging yet accessible (Dordio et al., 2024).

The integration of adaptivity and differentiation makes personalized learning highly effective. Adaptive learning systems provide real-time feedback and adjustments necessary to meet a student's immediate needs, while differentiation ensures that the broader educational experience is customized to the student's learning needs, abilities, and long-term goals. Several features of adaptive learning are particularly compatible with differentiated instruction:

- **Data-Driven Insights:** Adaptive learning systems continuously collect and analyze data on student performance, providing detailed insights into each student's strengths, weaknesses, and learning patterns. These insights inform differentiated instruction by helping teachers identify which students need more visual aids, additional practice, or alternative explanations (Frolovičeva, 2022).
- **Real-Time Feedback:** The real-time feedback offered by adaptive learning platforms helps teachers quickly identify when a student is struggling and why, allowing for immediate instructional adjustments such as additional scaffolding or enrichment activities. Differentiation is more effectively implemented because it is grounded in current, accurate data about student performance (Pane et al., 2017).
- **Customization of Learning Paths:** Adaptive learning systems allow for the customization of learning paths based on the student's performance and preferences. Differentiated instruction builds on this by aligning each student's path with their learning style and interests, making the educational experience more engaging and personalized (MATHia, Carnegie Learning).
- **Scalability of Personalized Interventions:** Adaptive learning systems can scale personalized interventions across a classroom or entire school, enabling teachers to provide differentiated instruction at scale without overwhelming them (Frolovičeva, 2022).
- **Continuous Adaptation:** Adaptive learning systems continuously monitor and adjust the learning experience, making differentiation a dynamic process that evolves in response to the student's progress. Teachers can use this continuous feedback loop to refine their strategies, ensuring that differentiation remains relevant and effective throughout the learning process (Pane et al., 2017).

In summary, merging adaptivity and differentiation forms the foundation of personalized learning, ensuring a uniquely tailored educational experience for each student while enhancing engagement and effectiveness. Integrated into experiential learning, it enables participation in real-world activities that are both relevant and impactful, paving the way for a deeply meaningful educational journey. Expanding on this foundation, AI and XR technologies further enhance the personalization of experiential learning strategies.

6.2.2 AI-XR Personalization of Experiential Learning

This section examines how AI and XR technologies can personalize various experiential learning approaches, including SBL, PBL, IBL, and CLIL. Through personalized adjustments and immersive experiences, AI and XR enhance student engagement, deepen understanding, and foster competency growth. In SBL, AI adapts scenarios in real-time based on student decisions, while XR immerses students in realistic environments, enhancing hands-on learning. In PBL, AI customizes project paths and provides real-time feedback, and XR simulates real-world settings, making projects more relevant and engaging. For IBL, AI tailors the complexity of research tasks, guiding students through personalized inquiry, while XR offers immersive experiences that bring abstract concepts to life. In CLIL, AI adjusts language and content instruction to individual proficiency levels, and XR creates culturally immersive environments that integrate language practice with content learning.

6.2.2.1 AI-XR Personalization of Scenario-Based Learning

SBL immerses students in realistic, context-rich scenarios that require them to apply knowledge and skills in practical, problem-solving situations. These scenarios often mirror real-life challenges, encouraging students to think critically and solve problems in contexts they might encounter outside the classroom. For example, in a digital literacy class, students might simulate managing a technology startup in sub-Saharan Africa, using digital tools to create marketing campaigns and develop a business plan. This immersive scenario allows students to apply economic concepts, develop entrepreneurial skills, and understand the complexities of operating in different cultural and economic environments. The effectiveness of SBL is rooted in its ability to simulate real-world environments, engage students in active learning, and provide immediate, context-specific feedback. These core tenets—realism, active learning, reflective practice, and adaptive feedback—are significantly enhanced through the integration of AI and XR technologies.

AI plays a pivotal role in SBL by dynamically adapting scenarios in real-time based on a student's actions, ensuring that each scenario remains relevant and appropriately challenging. For instance, in a medical training scenario, AI can simulate changes in a patient's condition, requiring students to make quick, informed decisions just as they would in a real clinical setting. This capability not only maintains student engagement but also promotes deeper understanding by constantly challenging learners at the appropriate level (Davé, 2023).

XR technologies—such as VR and AR—take the realism of SBL to the next level by immersing students in fully interactive, lifelike environments. In these settings, students are not merely passive recipients of information but active participants who must navigate complex scenarios that closely mirror real-world challenges. For example, in a crisis management simulation, one student might take on a leadership role, directing virtual team members through a disaster response, while another might focus on the technical aspects of the operation. Both students interact within the same scenario, but their experiences are tailored to their abilities and learning preferences, making the learning process more personalized and impactful (Paulsen et al., 2024).

The integration of AI supports active learning by continuously adjusting the scenario based on student performance. As students make decisions, AI algorithms modify the scenario's complexity, introducing new challenges or providing guidance as needed. This approach keeps students actively engaged and ensures they are consistently pushed to apply their knowledge at the edge of their capabilities (Davé, 2023). Additionally, XR environments allow students to interact with the scenario in a hands-on manner, such as manipulating virtual tools in an engineering simulation, providing practical experience in a safe, controlled setting (Pretolesi et al., 2023).

Reflective practice, a critical component of SBL, is also enhanced by AI and XR. After completing a scenario, AI can generate detailed, personalized feedback, highlighting areas of strength and suggesting improvements based on the student's performance. This data-driven feedback encourages students to reflect on their decisions and outcomes, deepening their understanding and facilitating continuous learning (Pretolesi et al., 2023). XR technologies complement this by allowing students to replay scenarios from different perspectives, enabling them to fully grasp the consequences of their actions (Paulsen et al., 2024).

Finally, AI's ability to provide real-time, adaptive feedback during scenarios is crucial for maintaining the personalized nature of SBL. As students navigate through scenarios, AI systems monitor their actions and offer immediate suggestions, corrections, or challenges, ensuring the learning experience is continuously tailored to their needs. In XR-based simulations, this feedback can be delivered in an immersive, interactive format, such as through a virtual assistant offering real-time guidance or environmental cues indicating shifts in scenario complexity. By integrating these technologies with the core principles of SBL, educators can create deeply personalized and effective learning environments that engage students and prepare them for real-world challenges with precision and adaptability.

6.2.2.2 AI-XR Personalization of Project-Based Learning
Project-based learning and service learning (SL) immerse students in real-world problems, requiring them to apply knowledge and skills over an extended period. Both approaches emphasize inquiry, collaboration, real-world application, and reflection, making learning deeply relevant and impactful (Bell, 2010). While PBL involves students working on extended projects to address real-world issues, SL can be conceived as a specific type of PBL that integrates meaningful community service. Through SL, students apply their skills to address societal needs, fostering personal growth, civic responsibility, and empathy (Kaye, 2010).

AI and XR technologies significantly enhance PBL and SL by providing immersive, interactive environments and personalized learning experiences. XR technologies, such as virtual reality (VR) and augmented reality (AR), create lifelike environments where students can explore complex topics. For instance, in a science project on marine ecosystems, students can use VR to dive into a virtual ocean, observing marine life and ecological interactions firsthand. This immersive experience deepens their understanding of the subject matter and allows for data gathering in a simulated, yet realistic, setting (Makransky & Mayer, 2022). Similarly, in a history project, VR can transport students to historical events, like walking through the streets of ancient Rome, offering a more engaging way to understand historical contexts and events (Bailenson, 2018).

AI supports PBL and SL by enabling personalized learning experiences through adaptive feedback and real-time data analysis. For instance, in a math-based project to optimize energy usage in a smart city simulation—a focus aligned with DIGICOMPASS's emphasis on technology and real-world application—AI tools like DreamBox Learning can adjust problem sets dynamically based on student performance. If a student struggles with calculating energy efficiency ratios, the AI provides step-by-step scaffolding, such as simplified examples or visual aids, before progressing to more complex equations.

Additionally, AI-powered tools like SimCityEDU and Esri's ArcGIS provide real-time feedback in service-learning projects. In an urban development project, SimCityEDU can simulate the social, economic, and environmental impacts of planning decisions, while ArcGIS allows students to analyze geographic data, such as traffic patterns or green space allocation. Meanwhile, platforms like Google's AutoML can assist students in analyzing real-world datasets, such as energy consumption patterns in their community. Using this data, students can propose practical, math-driven solutions, like reducing peak-hour energy demand, fostering both civic engagement and deeper mathematical understanding. By enabling students to visualize potential outcomes, refine their strategies, and make data-driven adjustments, AI tools ensure that learners are actively engaged and consistently challenged, promoting deeper learning and effective problem-solving.

Collaborative technologies such as MR platforms like Microsoft HoloLens and Spatial allow students to work together in shared virtual spaces, interacting with digital and physical objects. In engineering and design courses, tools like Unity Reflect and IrisVR Prospect enable teams to collaboratively manipulate and refine 3D models and prototypes, enhancing both the learning experience and the quality of their collaborative efforts.

Finally, reflective practice, a cornerstone of both PBL and SL, is enhanced by these technologies. After completing a project, AI can generate detailed feedback, helping students reflect on their learning process and the effectiveness of their solutions. XR technologies further this reflection by allowing students to revisit their projects from different perspectives, simulating the long-term impact of their work on the community and deepening their understanding of the broader implications of their contributions (Davé, 2023).

6.2.2.3 AI-XR Personalization of Inquiry-Based Learning
IBL is a student-centered approach that empowers learners to take charge of their learning process by posing questions, conducting research, and solving complex problems. Unlike PBL, which typically focuses on

completing a project with a clear end goal, or SBL, where students navigate predefined scenarios, IBL is more fluid and exploratory. It emphasizes curiosity, critical thinking, and the application of knowledge to real-world issues, with the learning journey being driven by the students' questions rather than a predetermined outcome. This method encourages learners to formulate research questions, gather and analyze data, and present their findings through a reflective and iterative process.

AI and XR technologies are revolutionizing IBL by tailoring the learning experience to individual needs and enhancing student engagement through immersive environments. AI plays a crucial role in personalizing the inquiry process. By analyzing student interactions and tracking progress, AI can offer real-time feedback and provide tailored resources that align with each learner's unique path. For example, AI-driven platforms like IBM Watson assist students in conducting research by identifying relevant sources, extracting key information, and generating insights that support evidence-based conclusions (Holmes et al., 2019). This personalized support allows students to delve deeper into their inquiries, fostering a more robust understanding of the subject matter.

XR technologies, such as VR and AR, further enhance IBL by creating immersive learning environments that bring inquiry-based projects to life. In a geography project, for instance, students might use VR to explore various ecosystems, observing environmental interactions firsthand. This immersive experience deepens their understanding of ecological principles and the impact of human activities, significantly boosting both engagement and retention (Makransky & Mayer, 2022). Similarly, in history inquiries, VR can transport students to ancient civilizations, allowing them to explore historical events and contexts as if they were there. This immersive approach not only makes history more tangible but also enhances students' ability to analyze and interpret historical data, offering a more engaging way to understand complex narratives (Bailenson, 2018).

The adaptability of AI in IBL extends to adjusting the level of inquiry based on student performance. Advanced students might be presented with more challenging questions, while others might receive foundational support. This ensures that each student is engaged at the appropriate level, making the learning experience more personalized and effective. XR technologies complement this by simulating complex phenomena or historical events, allowing students to engage with the material in a hands-on, immersive manner. For example, in a physics inquiry, VR can enable students to visualize and interact with forces and motion in a simulated environment, making abstract concepts more concrete and understandable through direct interaction.

By integrating AI and XR with the principles of IBL, educators can create learning experiences that are not only personalized and engaging but also highly effective in developing critical inquiry-based skills. These technologies empower students to take control of their educational journeys, encouraging deeper exploration and understanding of complex topics.

6.2.2.4 AI-XR Personalization of Content and Language Integrated Learning

CLIL is a distinctive educational approach that merges the teaching of subject content with language acquisition. Unlike other experiential learning approaches such as PBL, SBL, or IBL, CLIL uniquely combines the learning of subjects like science or history in another language. This dual focus not only promotes language proficiency but also enhances cognitive engagement and fosters intercultural understanding, making it a powerful tool for developing plurilingual and intercultural competence (Coyle et al., 2010).

In CLIL, students simultaneously absorb subject-specific content and develop language skills. This process demands high cognitive engagement, as learners must navigate complex material in a non-native language, which promotes deeper cognitive development. Moreover, CLIL is designed to enhance cultural awareness by integrating culturally relevant content, helping students appreciate the cultural contexts of the language they are learning. To support these challenges, scaffolding and support structures—such as visual aids, adapted texts, and interactive exercises—are essential for facilitating comprehension and ensuring that students can effectively manage the dual demands of language and content learning.

The integration of AI and XR technologies is revolutionizing CLIL by providing personalized learning experiences and immersive environments that enhance both language and content acquisition. AI tools are instrumental in offering personalized language support, a key feature in effective CLIL instruction. For example, AI-driven platforms like Duolingo and Babbel analyze a student's language proficiency and adapt content delivery to their level, offering real-time vocabulary support, grammar corrections, and personalized feedback. This adaptive approach helps students grasp both the language and the subject content more effectively, significantly improving language acquisition and retention (Holmes et al., 2019).

Moreover, AI's ability to adapt content complexity based on language proficiency ensures that students remain engaged and can successfully learn even complex subject matter. In a CLIL biology lesson, AI tools collaborate to provide personalized support for students at all proficiency levels. Flint enables teachers to create differentiated materials, such as simplified passages on "cell division" for beginners and advanced exercises on "mitosis and meiosis" for proficient learners. NotebookLM enhances accessibility by summarizing complex textbook chapters into concise, learner-friendly notes and offering explanations adapted to individual comprehension levels. Brisk Teaching assists educators by dynamically adjusting lesson plans, ensuring that instructional materials align with students' progress and language capabilities. Texthelp's Read&Write further supports beginners by simplifying text in real-time, while WolframAlpha breaks down advanced concepts into detailed, step-by-step explanations for more experienced learners.

XR technologies, such as VR, further enhance CLIL by creating immersive language environments that allow students to engage with content in the target language within lifelike settings. For example, VR can transport students to culturally significant locations, such as the streets of medieval Paris, where they can practice their French while exploring historical events. This type of immersive experience deepens both language skills and cultural understanding, making learning more engaging and effective (Bailenson, 2018). XR can also simulate real-world contexts that align with the subject matter. In a geography class focused on climate change, students might use VR to explore global ecosystems, interacting with the content in the target language. This immersive approach not only reinforces language learning but also makes the subject matter more tangible and relevant, enhancing both cognitive engagement and practical application (Makransky & Mayer, 2022).

Furthermore, XR environments support real-time interaction and feedback by allowing students to engage with virtual characters or peers in the target language. This immediate feedback on language use and content comprehension enhances both fluency and understanding. For instance, in an art history course taught in Italian, students might virtually visit the Uffizi Gallery, learning about artworks in Italian and applying their language skills in a culturally immersive context. This integration of language and content through immersive experiences helps students develop not only linguistic proficiency but also a deeper understanding of the cultural and historical contexts in which the language is used (Bailenson, 2018).

However, while AI tools are effective for personalized language practice, it is important to recognize their limitations. Mananay (2024) emphasizes that while AI can be highly effective in language teaching, it often falls short in providing the cultural context and nuanced feedback that human teachers excel at, particularly in areas like pragmatics and cultural subtleties. To overcome this limitation, language teachers are encouraged to integrate AI tools into their lesson plans strategically. By leveraging the data generated by AI tools, educators can tailor their instruction to meet individual needs, enhance student engagement, and complement AI-driven exercises with culturally relevant lessons that provide the context necessary for deeper understanding and meaningful communication.

By integrating AI and XR technologies with the core principles of CLIL, educators can create personalized, immersive learning environments that effectively support both content and language acquisition. These technologies not only enhance cognitive development and cultural awareness but also prepare students to apply their language skills in real-world contexts while mastering subject-specific content, making CLIL a powerful tool within the DIGICOMPASS framework.

6.2.3 AI-XR Personalization of Inclusive Practices

AI and XR technologies play a transformative role in personalizing inclusive educational practices, particularly culturally responsive education (CRE), universal design for learning (UDL), and social-emotional learning (SEL). These practices share a common goal of creating an educational environment that is accessible, equitable, and supportive for all students. What makes them inclusive is their commitment to addressing the diverse needs of learners by recognizing cultural backgrounds, providing multiple means of engagement, and fostering emotional and social development. CRE focuses on embedding students' cultural identities into the learning process, ensuring that education is relevant and meaningful. UDL aims to remove barriers to learning by offering flexible ways to access content, engage with material, and demonstrate understanding. SEL prioritizes the development of emotional intelligence and interpersonal skills, which are crucial for both personal and academic success. Together, these practices ensure that every student, regardless of background or ability, can thrive in an educational setting. When enhanced by AI and XR, these inclusive practices not only support but also amplify the effectiveness of the experiential learning approaches discussed earlier, making education more responsive, personalized, and engaging.

6.2.3.1 AI-XR Personalization of Culturally Responsive Education
CRE integrates students' cultural backgrounds into the learning process, fostering an inclusive environment that enhances engagement and connection. Key tenets of CRE include cultural awareness and inclusion, ensuring that diverse backgrounds are reflected in the curriculum to make content relevant and meaningful (Gay, 2018). Equitable access to learning focuses on adapting materials and methods to align with students' cultural contexts (Banks, 2015). Student-centered instruction encourages students to share their perspectives, creating an engaging classroom environment, while building cultural competence aims to help students understand and appreciate different cultures, fostering empathy and global citizenship (Ladson-Billings, 1995).

AI and XR technologies significantly enhance CRE by providing personalized and immersive learning experiences. AI-driven platforms can tailor educational content to reflect individual cultural backgrounds, ensuring engagement with meaningful materials. For example, AI-powered educational tools like IBM's Watson Education can adapt content based on cultural contexts, supporting both content comprehension and cultural awareness (Holmes et al., 2019). AI can also create learning paths that highlight contributions from diverse cultures, guiding students through culturally relevant curricula and enhancing their sense of belonging.

XR technologies, such as Google Expeditions and VR simulations from Stanford's Virtual Human Interaction Lab, provide students with immersive experiences that allow them to explore different parts of the world from their classrooms. These tools enable virtual tours of significant locations like the Great Wall of China or the pyramids of Egypt, as well as empathy-building experiences that help students understand different cultural and social perspectives (Bailenson, 2018). VR can also simulate real-world scenarios, helping students develop empathy and cultural competence by interacting with people from diverse backgrounds, which is essential for teaching students to navigate cultural norms and language barriers effectively.

In rural areas of sub-Saharan Africa, mobile learning during school disruptions has successfully used AI-driven content to maintain literacy and engagement. These programs, tailored to local contexts, include culturally relevant stories and examples, making education more relatable and effective for students in remote areas (Kizilcec et al., 2021). Additionally, projects like the Digital Literacy Project in Kenya have improved learning outcomes by integrating digital tools and culturally relevant content into the curriculum, addressing the educational needs of remote communities (Ooko, 2023). By integrating AI and XR technologies, CRE can create personalized, immersive learning environments that reflect students' diverse cultural backgrounds. These technologies make learning more relevant and engaging while fostering cultural competence, empathy, and global citizenship.

6.2.3.2 AI-XR Personalization of Universal Design for Learning

UDL is an educational framework designed to make learning accessible and effective for all students by offering multiple means of engagement, representation, and action/expression (Meyer et al., 2014). The 3.0 version emphasizes the importance of flexibility and technology integration, ensuring that diverse learners, including those with disabilities, can fully participate in the educational process (CAST, 2024).

"Multiple Means of Engagement" acknowledges that learners are motivated by different factors, including individual abilities, interests, and prior experiences. AI enhances this by personalizing content delivery to align with each student's unique needs. AI-driven platforms, such as Knewton Alta, adjust content dynamically, modifying difficulty levels or presenting material in diverse formats to sustain engagement. For instance, if the system detects a decline in a student's interaction, it might switch from text-based explanations to interactive simulations or gamified quizzes, ensuring the material remains engaging and accessible. This adaptability helps maintain motivation and supports a more effective learning experience.

"Multiple Means of Representation" involves presenting information in diverse ways to meet varied learning needs and ensure accessibility for all learners. XR technologies, particularly VR, significantly enhance this principle by providing immersive and interactive learning experiences that combine visual, auditory, and kinesthetic modalities. For example, in a science lesson, students might use VR to explore a 3D model of the human body, examining organs and systems through touch, sound, and visuals. This approach supports diverse ways of processing information and makes abstract concepts more concrete and understandable, benefiting a wide range of learners.

"Multiple Means of Action and Expression" focuses on offering students various ways to demonstrate their learning. AI tools, such as Microsoft 365 Copilot, support this by providing personalized suggestions and diverse options for students to showcase their understanding. For instance, in a history lesson, an AI system might guide a student to create an infographic summarizing key events using Canva for Education, develop a video presentation, or write a detailed report. Microsoft 365 Copilot can assist by generating outlines, formatting documents, or creating visual aids like charts, helping students express their knowledge in ways that align with their strengths and abilities.

Building on these principles, AI tools like Lingvist or Ellii continuously track student progress, dynamically adapting language activities to match individual learning needs. For instance, in a language lesson, Lingvist might simplify vocabulary and grammar exercises for beginners while providing advanced learners with challenging texts that incorporate idiomatic expressions or complex structures, ensuring all students are appropriately challenged and engaged. For example, in a language lesson, AI might adapt reading comprehension exercises by simplifying vocabulary for beginners or introducing more complex texts for advanced learners, ensuring that every student is appropriately challenged. Similarly, XR technologies expand UDL's scope by enabling experiential learning opportunities, such as virtual field trips that can be customized to meet diverse learning needs (Ibáñez & Delgado-Kloos, 2018). For instance, in a geography class, students could use VR to explore global ecosystems, with the experience tailored to focus on aspects such as biodiversity, climate patterns, or human impact, depending on their learning abilities and interests. By integrating AI and XR technologies, UDL 3.0 has the potential to provide learners, regardless of their needs or preferences, with personalized and inclusive educational experiences.

6.2.3.3 AI-XR Personalization of Social-Emotional Learning

SEL is a vital educational approach that focuses on the development of students' emotional intelligence, self-awareness, empathy, and interpersonal skills. These competencies are essential for fostering a positive school environment and preparing students to navigate social and emotional challenges throughout their lives. SEL's key tenets—self-awareness, self-management, social awareness, relationship skills, and responsible decision-making—provide a comprehensive framework for cultivating these abilities.

Self-awareness involves understanding one's own emotions, strengths, and limitations, which in turn influences behavior and thought patterns. Self-management extends this understanding by equipping students with the skills to regulate their emotions, thoughts, and behaviors across different situations, including managing stress, controlling impulses, and setting and achieving goals. Social awareness emphasizes the importance of empathy and understanding others, particularly those from diverse backgrounds and cultures. This tenet also involves recognizing social norms and ethical behavior. Relationship skills are crucial for establishing and maintaining healthy and rewarding relationships through effective communication, active listening, cooperation, and conflict resolution. Finally, responsible decision-making is the ability to make ethical, constructive choices regarding personal and social behavior, considering the well-being of oneself and others while evaluating the consequences of various actions.

AI and XR technologies offer significant opportunities to enhance and personalize SEL by tailoring interventions to meet individual needs, creating immersive environments that foster empathy and understanding, and providing real-time feedback to support emotional and social development. AI plays a critical role in SEL by providing personalized emotional support and data-driven interventions. For instance, AI can monitor students' emotional states using natural language processing (NLP) and sentiment analysis during their interactions with digital platforms. AI-driven platforms can detect when a student is feeling frustrated or anxious and respond with supportive messages or suggest relaxation techniques.

Additionally, AI can adjust the learning environment to reduce stress by modifying the difficulty of tasks or offering encouraging feedback, which supports students' self-management and emotional regulation (Ayeni et al., 2024). AI can also analyze patterns in student behavior and performance to identify those who may require additional emotional or social support. For example, if a student consistently displays signs of disengagement or distress during certain activities, AI can alert educators, who can then intervene with appropriate SEL strategies tailored to that student's needs (Luckin et al., 2016; Kokku et al., 2018).

XR technologies, particularly VR, also play a transformative role in SEL by creating immersive experiences that allow students to "step into someone else's shoes." For example, a VR scenario might simulate the experience of being a refugee, helping students develop empathy and social awareness by understanding the challenges faced by others. These experiences deepen students' understanding of diverse perspectives, fostering greater empathy and social consciousness (Walker & Venker Weidenbenner, 2019). XR can also simulate real-world social interactions in a controlled, safe environment, allowing students to practice relationship skills such as communication, conflict resolution, and teamwork. For instance, students might use VR to navigate a virtual workplace, learning how to interact with colleagues and manage conflicts. These simulations provide a safe space for students to experiment with different social behaviors and receive real-time feedback on their actions (Zhang et al., 2024).

Furthermore, XR can support SEL by providing immersive environments for mindfulness and relaxation. Students can use VR to enter calming virtual spaces where they can practice mindfulness exercises or guided meditations, helping them develop self-management skills like stress reduction and emotional regulation (Zhang et al., 2024). In practical applications, AI-driven SEL platforms might monitor a student's progress in an SEL program, analyzing data to identify areas where the student needs further development. For example, if AI detects a pattern of stress during group activities, it could recommend targeted exercises in communication and stress management, helping the student build stronger relationship skills. Similarly, in a social studies class, students might use VR to experience life from the perspective of individuals in different cultural or socioeconomic situations. This immersive experience can help students build social awareness and empathy, key components of SEL.

By integrating AI and XR technologies with the core tenets of social-emotional learning, educators can create personalized, immersive learning environments that support emotional and social development. These technologies not only enhance students' self-awareness, empathy, and relationship skills but also provide a more engaging and effective way to cultivate the social and emotional competencies needed for success in both school and life.

6.2.4 *The Synergy of AI-XR Personalized and Experiential Learning*

The integration of AI and XR technologies within personalized and experiential learning, particularly through CLIL, PBL, IBL, and SBL, aligns seamlessly with the DIGICOMPASS framework's foundational pillars. Central to this framework is digital literacy, the guiding star that ensures students are proficient in navigating, evaluating, and creating within digital environments. This constant focus on digital literacy is complemented by inclusive practices such as CRE, UDL, and SEL. These practices are not only interconnected but also flexible, enabling educators to dynamically adapt the curriculum based on real-time feedback from AI tools. This adaptability ensures that the curriculum meets the evolving needs of students and allows educators to address emerging global challenges—such as climate change or digital ethics—by integrating these critical topics into the existing framework.

By fostering a blend of digital literacy, intercultural competence, and ethical decision-making, DIGICOMPASS prepares students for lifelong learning and responsible citizenship in an increasingly digitally interconnected world. The framework's flexibility ensures that students remain future-ready, capable of adapting to new technologies and societal demands.

Multiliteracies—including digital, intercultural, ethical, creative, and global literacies—are central to this approach, especially in addressing pressing global issues. For instance, integrating global literacy into CLIL projects enables students to engage with challenges like sustainability or public health in culturally informed and ethically grounded ways. AI and XR technologies empower students to interact with content in multimodal forms, such as immersive VR experiences, interactive cultural simulations, and dynamic data visualizations. This comprehensive approach ensures that students are not just well-rounded but also proactive in tackling global challenges. Below are some examples that illustrate the synergy between AI-XR technologies, personalized and experiential learning approaches, and inclusive practices:

- **CLIL with PBL, UDL, and Digital Literacy**: In a CLIL-based project on renewable energy, AI personalizes language content to match individual proficiency levels, while XR immerses students in virtual tours of renewable energy facilities worldwide. This approach aligns with UDL by providing multiple means of engagement and representation, ensuring all students can fully participate and understand both the language and content. Digital literacy is developed as students use various digital tools to explore, create, and present their findings, enhancing their ability to critically evaluate and communicate information (Ibáñez & Delgado-Kloos, 2018).

(continued)

(continued)
- **CLIL with SBL, SEL, and Ethical Literacy**: In a CLIL scenario centered on climate policy negotiation, students engage in a virtual simulation of international negotiations. AI adjusts language complexity and scenario challenges based on student performance, while XR immerses them in a multilingual, culturally diverse environment. This integration supports SEL by fostering empathy and collaboration, essential for ethical decision-making and social awareness. Ethical literacy is enhanced as students grapple with the moral and cultural implications of their decisions within the simulation, learning to navigate the complexities of global citizenship (Bailenson, 2018).
- **CLIL with IBL, CRE, and Intercultural Literacy**: In an IBL project focused on global health issues, AI supports personalized language instruction within a CLIL framework, while XR allows students to virtually explore healthcare systems across different countries. This approach integrates CRE by embedding culturally relevant health practices into the learning process, ensuring that students develop both linguistic and cultural competence. Intercultural literacy is deepened as students engage with diverse cultural perspectives, analyze global health data, and communicate findings in multiple languages, enhancing their ability to operate in a global context (Holmes et al., 2019).

Though DIGICOMPASS has yet to be implemented, its potential impact can be projected based on the strengths of its components. By intertwining AI-XR with inclusive and experiential learning strategies, DIGICOMPASS could significantly improve student outcomes, particularly in critical thinking, collaboration, and global competence. The framework also offers vast opportunities for research and development in educational technology. Future research could include pilot studies, cross-cultural comparisons, and longitudinal research that tracks student progress over time, providing data to refine and optimize the framework. This approach not only has the potential to validate the efficacy of DIGICOMPASS but also positions it as a cutting-edge educational model for the twenty-first century.

The powerful synergy of AI-XR personalization within CLIL, PBL, SBL, IBL, UDL, SEL, CRE, and multiliteracies makes education adaptive, inclusive, culturally relevant, and emotionally supportive, maximizing student engagement and success across diverse learning environments. This integrated approach equips students with the necessary skills and competencies to thrive in a digitally connected and culturally diverse world, establishing DIGICOMPASS as a forward-thinking framework capable of addressing the challenges of contemporary education and beyond.

6.3 DIGICOMPASS IN ACTION: A HIGH SCHOOL SEMESTER MODULE

6.3.1 Climate Change and Environmental Science (Science and World Languages)

6.3.1.1 Course Description
This 11th-grade interdisciplinary module explores climate change and environmental science through a plurilingual approach, combining scientific inquiry with language learning. Students will study the causes and effects of climate change, explore ecosystems via VR, and analyze global environmental policies while developing proficiency in a target language. The course emphasizes plurilingual and pluricultural competence, preparing students to navigate and mediate between different languages and cultures. Activities include researching cultural responses to climate change, engaging in scenario-based problem-solving, and collaborating on an environmental action plan for a specific region. Digital storytelling is integrated throughout the course, allowing students to document their findings and reflections creatively. The module culminates in a final project where students present their research and insights through digital storytelling, demonstrating their scientific understanding, cultural awareness, and multilingual communication skills.

6.3.1.2 Pedagogical Approaches

- **CLIL** is utilized to teach climate change and environmental science through the target language, enabling students to acquire scientific concepts such as the greenhouse effect, carbon cycles, and renewable energy while building relevant vocabulary and language skills. By

reading and discussing scientific articles, watching documentaries, and engaging in debates—all in the target language—students deepen their understanding of both the content and the language. CLIL fosters cultural and intercultural competence by integrating environmental content from diverse regions, allowing students to explore how different communities are affected by and respond to climate change. Digital storytelling will be used as a tool to document these insights, encouraging students to create narratives that connect scientific data with cultural perspectives.
- **SBL** immerses students in realistic situations where they must apply both scientific and linguistic knowledge to address environmental challenges. For example, students might develop a sustainability plan for a community threatened by rising sea levels, integrating scientific data and cultural considerations. Digital storytelling will be an integral part of this process, enabling students to present their sustainability plans creatively, using multimedia tools to convey their findings and proposed solutions. This approach fosters critical thinking as students navigate complex issues like balancing economic development with environmental protection, making informed decisions, and presenting their solutions in the target language while reflecting on the broader impact of their choices.

6.3.1.3 *Inclusive Practices*

- **SEL** is woven throughout the module to support students' emotional and social development. In group activities and discussions, students practice empathy, active listening, and teamwork. For instance, during scenario-based tasks, students work together to address the needs of different stakeholders affected by climate change, developing their ability to navigate complex social dynamics. Digital storytelling projects also incorporate SEL by encouraging students to express their thoughts and emotions about environmental issues creatively.
- **UDL** principles ensure that all students can engage with the content. The module provides multiple means of representation (e.g., visual aids and bilingual texts), engagement (e.g., interactive scenarios and debates), and expression (e.g., multimedia presentations and written reports). Adaptive technologies are used to adjust the complexity of materials, ensuring that students at different language proficiency levels can fully participate. Digital storytelling, supported by tools

like Adobe Spark and Canva, allows students to showcase their learning in various formats.
- **CRE** is central to the module, ensuring that students' cultural backgrounds are respected and integrated into the curriculum. Students explore how climate change impacts their own communities and those around the world, discussing these impacts in the target language. Digital storytelling enables them to incorporate their cultural knowledge into their projects, fostering a deeper understanding of global environmental challenges and how different cultures respond to them.

6.3.1.4 Technologies, Multiliteracies, and Personalized Learning

- **AI-Driven Adaptive Learning Platforms:** Platforms like MEL Science VR, Smart Sparrow, and Century Tech personalize content delivery by analyzing student performance and adjusting task complexity in real-time. These tools support pragmatic competence and digital literacy by addressing individual knowledge gaps and adapting to evolving needs. For example, a student struggling with environmental science concepts might receive simplified explanations or interactive tutorials, while advanced students could be challenged with deeper analytical tasks or scenario-based simulations. Similarly, tools like Diffit and Quizlet use AI to create tailored flashcards, quizzes, and reading materials that align with each student's language proficiency and understanding of scientific concepts.
- **VR and AI-Enhanced Storytelling Tools:** Tools like ENGAGE VR, ClassVR, and CoSpaces Edu enable immersive, personalized experiences where students explore environmental scenarios aligned with their learning goals. For instance, Google Earth VR allows students to examine the effects of rising sea levels in coastal regions, while ThingLink lets them create interactive, multimedia-rich maps to illustrate the impacts of climate change on specific ecosystems. Additionally, tools like Floreo VR provide tiered virtual experiences, ensuring that both beginners and advanced learners can engage meaningfully with the content. These tools foster global literacy through real-world insights, ethical literacy by prompting reflection on environmental ethics, and intercultural literacy by immersing students in diverse cultural perspectives.
- **Digital Media Tools:** Creative platforms like WeVideo, Adobe Express, and Canva for Education empower students to craft digital

storytelling projects that effectively communicate their findings. These tools enhance digital literacy by teaching students to navigate and evaluate digital tools, and they foster creative literacy by encouraging them to produce original, multimedia-rich content. For example, students might use WeVideo to create a documentary detailing the environmental policies of a specific region, incorporating visuals, narration, and subtitles in the target language. Beginners can use Canva to create visually appealing infographics with scaffolded support, while advanced students develop complex multimedia presentations.
- **Differentiated Instruction:** This module integrates tiering, scaffolding, and choice-based learning to address students' diverse proficiency in science and language. A student advanced in science but a beginner in the target language might work with bilingual resources, scaffolded tasks, or tools like Diffit to generate simplified readings. Conversely, a student proficient in the target language but less familiar with scientific concepts might use visual aids, guided problem-solving activities, or ThingLink to build foundational knowledge. Flexible project formats—such as podcasts, digital posters, or video documentaries—allow all students to showcase their learning in ways that align with their strengths. For instance, beginners might create simple infographics, intermediate learners could produce narrated podcasts, and advanced learners might craft detailed VR simulations using CoSpaces Edu or develop in-depth video documentaries.

6.3.1.5 CEFR Levels, Activities, and Competences

- **Listening (A2–B1):**
  - **A2:** Students understand simple, factual information during lectures and discussions, especially in familiar contexts like basic climate change concepts and ecosystem introductions.
  - **B1:** They comprehend key points in more detailed discussions, such as those involving climate change scenarios, data collection methods, and the implications of environmental changes.
- **Reading (A2–B1):**
  - **A2:** Focuses on understanding the main ideas in simple articles related to environmental topics, such as short descriptions of ecosystems or the basic effects of climate change.
  - **B1:** Students begin to analyze and interpret more detailed texts, such as articles on climate change, environmental policies, or basic

GIS data reports. They can extract relevant information and summarize it effectively.
- **Speaking (A2–B1):**
  - **A2:** Involves basic exchanges of information, such as describing familiar environmental scenarios or summarizing simple texts. Students might discuss the effects of climate change in their own community using simple language structures.
  - **B1:** Students engage in discussions and presentations of research findings, articulating ideas with some fluency. They can explain environmental scenarios, present findings on cultural responses to climate change, and participate in debates on sustainable practices.
- **Writing (A2–B1):**
  - **A2:** Tasks focus on clear, simple communication, such as summarizing research or drafting short reports on climate change impacts or simple environmental action plans.
  - **B1:** Involves producing coherent paragraphs and reports on environmental topics, using appropriate vocabulary and structure. Students might write short essays or reports on environmental policies or their research findings.
- **Interaction (A2–B1):**
  - **A2:** Includes participation in basic role-plays and group discussions, using simple language to express ideas and collaborate on environmental projects. Students may work together to create a basic environmental action plan.
  - **B1:** Students take on more interactive roles, contributing effectively in group tasks and managing conversations. They might lead a group discussion on the cultural impacts of climate change or collaborate on a project to model environmental solutions.
- **Mediation (B1):**
  - **B1:** Students summarize environmental information for peers, facilitate discussions, and explain straightforward concepts in the target language. They might mediate a discussion between groups with differing viewpoints on an environmental issue, helping to clarify and translate ideas.
- **Plurilingual and Pluricultural Competence (B1):**
  - **B1:** Students use their linguistic repertoire to navigate multilingual sources and compare cultural responses to environmental issues. They might compare how different communities are

affected by climate change and reflect on these differences in discussions or written reports.
- **Pragmatic Competence (B1):**
  - **B1:** Involves structuring communication logically in both spoken and written forms, particularly in data reporting and scenario discussions. Students ensure clarity and coherence in their presentations and digital storytelling projects, tailoring their language to the audience.

6.3.1.6 Course Overview
- **Weeks 1–2: Introduction** (Table 6.1)
  - **Topics:** Basics of climate change, introduction to ecosystems, foundational vocabulary building.
  - **Activities:**
    Lectures and discussions supported by Diffit for Teachers to create leveled reading materials.
    VR exploration of ecosystems using Google Earth VR and Labster, where students can simulate interactions within an ecosystem to visualize concepts like food chains and biodiversity.
    Digital portfolios using Adobe Express or Canva for Education to organize reflections and vocabulary lists.
  - **Assessment:**
    Initial quizzes generated by Quizlet to reinforce key terms.
    VR and Labster simulation reflections submitted in digital portfolios.
    Evaluation of portfolio setup using differentiated prompts.
  - **CEFR Level: A2–B1**
    A2: Understanding simple, factual information during lectures and discussions.
    B1: Engaging in discussions and describing scenarios using relevant vocabulary.
- **Weeks 3–6: Data Collection and Analysis**
  - **Topics:** Methods for collecting environmental data, using GIS for analysis.

Table 6.1 Weeks 1–2 lesson plan: introduction to climate change and environmental science

Lesson phase	Activities and instructions	Teaching roles	Description	Differentiation and EdTech tools
Objectives	• Introduce basic concepts of climate change (e.g., greenhouse effect, carbon cycle) • Develop relevant vocabulary in the target language • Use VR and digital tools for immersive learning • Introduce digital storytelling as a method for presenting findings • Understand foundational climate change concepts, practice basic language skills, enhance digital literacy	T1: Science Specialist T2: Language Specialist	• Establishes key themes and learning goals for the module • Prepares students for engagement through technology, language, and storytelling	• Smart Sparrow for adaptive content • Diffit for creating leveled reading materials • Google Classroom for task management and digital portfolio organization
Introduction to Climate Change (15 min)	• Discuss climate change concepts (e.g., causes and effects of greenhouse gases) • Introduce relevant vocabulary in the target language • Show short videos or animations explaining the greenhouse effect	T1: Science Specialist	• Introduces foundational climate change concepts using multimedia resources • Engages students in an interactive discussion	• Edpuzzle for interactive video-based discussion • Nearpod for real-time polls and vocabulary practice • Diffit for leveled text-handouts

(continued)

Table 6.1 (continued)

Lesson phase	Activities and instructions	Teaching roles	Description	Differentiation and EdTech tools
VR Exploration of Ecosystems (20 min)	• Students explore ecosystems using Google Earth VR to observe climate change impacts • Use Labster to simulate ecosystem interactions • Complete observation worksheets in the target language	T1: Science Specialist T2: Language Specialist	• T1 covers scientific content, and T2 supports language practice • Promotes hands-on exploration and reflection	• Google Earth VR for immersive exploration • Labster for interactive simulations • Nearpod for guided observation activities
Lecture and Discussion (20 min)	• Provide a brief lecture on ecosystems' role in climate regulation • Facilitate a discussion about students' VR experiences and observations	T1: Science Specialist T2: Language Specialist	• Connects theoretical knowledge with hands-on VR experiences • Encourages vocabulary use in meaningful discussions	• Nearpod for interactive polls and questions • Edpuzzle for video lecture support • Quizlet for live vocabulary quizzes
Break (10 min)				
Introduction to Digital Portfolios (15 min)	• Explain the purpose of digital portfolios for documenting learning • Introduce digital storytelling as tool for sharing insights • Show examples of digital portfolios	T2: Language Specialist	• Prepares students for ongoing documentation and storytelling • Emphasizes portfolio use as a tool for communication	• Google Classroom for organizing digital portfolio templates • Adobe Express for creating visually engaging portfolios • Canva for designing storytelling elements

(continued)

Table 6.1 (continued)

Lesson phase	Activities and instructions	Teaching roles	Description	Differentiation and EdTech tools
Setting up Digital Portfolios (20 min)	• Students begin creating digital portfolios, documenting VR exploration and initial reflections • Brainstorm ideas for digital storytelling projects	T1: Science Specialist T2: Language Specialist	• Provides hands-on support for portfolio setup and storytelling. • Fosters creativity in initial project planning.	• Adobe Express for portfolio creation • Canva for visual design • Diffit for language scaffolding in reflections
Vocabulary Practice (20 min)	• Use adaptive learning tools to practice relevant climate change vocabulary in the target language • Conduct short quizzes to strengthen vocabulary and key concepts	T2: Language Specialist	• Focuses on strengthening key vocabulary • Uses digital tools for personalized learning experiences	• Smart Sparrow for adaptive vocabulary exercises • Quizlet for interactive flashcards, matching games, and live quizzes
Reflection and Wrap-up (10 min)	• Write a short reflection on what was learned about climate change and its effects on ecosystems • Share reflections in small groups	T1: Science Specialist T2: Language Specialist	• Promotes learning through reflection and collaboration • Enhances communication and teamwork	• Google Classroom for submitting reflections • Nearpod for collaborative discussion and group sharing

(continued)

Table 6.1 (continued)

Lesson phase	Activities and instructions	Teaching roles	Description	Differentiation and EdTech tools
Homework/ Extended Learning	• Research a specific ecosystem and write a paragraph on how climate change affects it • Outline ideas for digital storytelling projects • Submit findings to the digital portfolio	T1: Science Specialist T2: Language Specialist	• Encourages independent research and deeper engagement • Prepares students for the digital storytelling component	• Google Classroom for assignment submission and feedback • Adobe Express for expanding portfolios and storytelling elements

- **Activities:**
    Field trips for data collection using mobile GIS apps like ArcGIS Field Maps.
    GIS data analysis supplemented by Labster's data interpretation simulations, providing students with hands-on practice in interpreting environmental data.
    Language practice supported by NotebookLM for summarizing findings and improving target language use.
- **Assessment:**
    Formative assessments through digital portfolios documenting data collection and analysis, including Labster simulation outcomes.
    Feedback sessions guided by Khanmigo Teacher Tools to address gaps in science or language understanding.
- **CEFR Level: A2–B1**
    A2: Participating in basic field activities, understanding and using GIS tools with guidance.
    B1: Practicing data reporting in the target language and conducting simple analysis.
- **Weeks 7–10: Scenario Development and Cultural Analysis**
    - **Topics:** Creating environmental models, cultural impacts of climate change.
    - **Activities:**

Developing environmental models with CoSpaces Edu to build VR simulations of climate scenarios.

Cultural analysis tasks supported by differentiated texts from Diffit for Teachers.

Researching climate policies through Labster's interactive climate change scenarios, where students experiment with policy changes and see simulated impacts on environments and communities.

Scenario creation using ThingLink to combine scientific data and cultural insights.
- **Assessment:**

Feedback on models and scenarios with support from Khanmigo Teacher Tools.

Peer reviews of cultural integration and storytelling elements.
- **CEFR Level: B1**

B1: Describing and discussing cultural impacts and creating simple models/scenarios.
- **Weeks 11-13: Finalizing Digital Stories and Preparing Presentations**
  - **Topics:** Refining digital storytelling projects, presentation skills.
  - **Activities:**

  Finalizing digital stories using multimedia tools like WeVideo, Adobe Express, or Canva for Education.

  Presentation practice with ENGAGE VR, simulating real-world audiences for rehearsals.

  Refining content and language with AI support from Magic School AI and NotebookLM.
  - **Assessment:**

  Peer and self-assessments of digital stories.

  Formative evaluations of multimedia content and storytelling quality.
  - **CEFR Level: B1**

  B1: Creating coherent digital stories, presenting ideas clearly, and interacting effectively in collaborative sessions.
- **Week 14-15: Final Presentations and Assessment**
  - **Activities:**

  Final presentations using multimedia tools, class discussions, feedback, and reflection activities. Students present their digital

storytelling projects, demonstrating their scientific knowledge, cultural insights, and language proficiency.
- **Assessment:**
Summative assessment of digital storytelling projects and presentations, final review of digital portfolios.
- **CEFR Level: B1**
B1: Delivering presentations that synthesize research findings and participating in reflective discussions.

6.4 Conclusion

The integration of AI and XR technologies within the DIGICOMPASS framework represents a significant advancement in personalized and experiential learning. By leveraging adaptive learning systems, immersive simulations, and real-time data analytics, educators can create highly customized and engaging educational experiences that cater to diverse student needs. These technologies not only enhance the effectiveness of pedagogical approaches like SBL, PBL, and IBL but also ensure inclusivity through frameworks like UDL and CRE. The practical modules and co-teaching guidelines provided in DIGICOMPASS offer a clear roadmap for implementing these technologies effectively, ensuring that educators can navigate this complex landscape with confidence. As AI and XR technologies continue to evolve, they hold the potential to transform education, making it more responsive, inclusive, and impactful, while also addressing ethical considerations and the need for continuous professional development among educators.

References

Ayeni, O. O., Al Hamad, N. M., Chisom, O. N., Osawaru, B., & Adewusi, O. E. (2024). AI in education: A review of personalized learning and educational technology. *GSC Advanced Research and Reviews, 18*(2), 261–271. https://gsconlinepress.com/journals/gscarr/sites/default/files/GSCARR-2024-0062.pdf

Bailenson, J. (2018). *Experience on demand: What virtual reality is, how it works, and what it can do.* W. W. Norton & Company.

Banks, J. A. (2015). *Cultural diversity and education: Foundations, curriculum, and teaching.* Routledge.

Bell, S. (2010). Project-based learning for the 21st century: Skills for the future. *The Clearing House: A Journal of Educational Strategies, Issues and Ideas, 83*(2), 39–43.

CAST. (2024). *Universal design for learning guidelines version 3.0.* CAST. https://udlguidelines.cast.org

Coyle, D., Hood, P., & Marsh, D. (2010). *CLIL: Content and language integrated learning.* Cambridge University Press.

Davé, P. (2023). *The revolutionary intersection of AI and immersive learning in higher education.* Emerging Technologies Consortium, Columbia University. https://etc.cuit.columbia.edu/news/revolutionary-intersection-ai-and-immersive-learning-higher-education

Dordio, A., Lancho, E., Merchán, M. J., & Merchán, P. (2024). Cultural heritage as a didactic resource through extended reality: A systematic review of the literature. *Multimodal Technologies and Interaction, 8*(7), 58. https://doi.org/10.3390/mti8070058

Froloviĉeva, V. (2022). Differentiated learning in the context of immersive technologies. *International Journal of Smart Education and Urban Society (IJSEUS), 13*(1), 1–10.

Gay, G. (2018). *Culturally responsive teaching: Theory, research, and practice.* Teachers College Press.

Herrington, J., & Oliver, R. (2000). An instructional design framework for authentic learning environments. *Educational Technology Research and Development, 48*(3), 23–48.

Holmes, W., Bialik, M., & Fadel, C. (2019). *Artificial intelligence in education: Promises and implications for teaching and learning.* Center for Curriculum Redesign.

Ibáñez, M.-B., & Delgado-Kloos, C. (2018). Augmented reality for STEM learning: A systematic review. *Computers & Education, 123*, 109–123.

Kaye, C. B. (2010). *The complete guide to service learning: Proven, practical ways to engage students in civic responsibility, academic curriculum, & social action.* Free Spirit Publishing.

Kizilcec, R. F., Chen, M., Jasińska, K. K., Madaio, M., & Ogan, A. (2021). Mobile learning during school disruptions in sub-Saharan Africa. *AERA Open, 7*, 23328584211014860. https://journals.sagepub.com/doi/10.1177/23328584211014860

Kokku, R., Sundararajan, S., Dey, P., Sindhgatta, R., Nitta, S., & Sengupta, B. (2018). Augmenting classrooms with AI for personalized education. In *2018 IEEE International Conference on Acoustics, Speech and Signal Processing (ICASSP)* (pp. 6976–6980). IEEE.

Kokotsaki, D., Menzies, V., & Wiggins, A. (2016). Project-based learning: A review of the literature. *Improving Schools, 19*(3), 267–277.

Kolb, D. A. (2015). *Experiential learning: Experience as the source of learning and development*. Pearson Education.

Ladson-Billings, G. (1995). Toward a theory of culturally relevant pedagogy. *American Educational Research Journal, 32*(3), 465–491.

Lim-Ratnam, C. (2019). Curriculum leadership. In B. Wong, S. Hairon, & P. T. Ng (Eds.), *School leadership and educational change in Singapore* (pp. 31–50). Springer. https://doi.org/10.1007/978-3-319-74746-0_3

Luckin, R., Holmes, W., Griffiths, M., & Forcier, L. B. (2016). *Intelligence unleashed: An argument for AI in education*. Pearson. https://www.pearson.com/content/dam/corporate/global/pearson-dot-com/files/innovation/Intelligence-Unleashed-Publication.pdf

Makransky, G., & Mayer, R. E. (2022). Benefits of taking a virtual field trip in immersive virtual reality: Evidence for the immersion principle in multimedia learning. *Educational Psychology Review, 34*(1), 71–92. https://www.researchgate.net/publication/359649690_Benefits_of_Taking_a_Virtual_Field_Trip_in_Immersive_Virtual_Reality_Evidence_for_the_Immersion_Principle_in_Multimedia_Learning

Mananay, J. A. (2024). Integrating artificial intelligence (AI) in language teaching: Effectiveness, challenges, and strategies. *International Journal of Learning, Teaching and Educational Research, 23*(9), 361–382. https://www.researchgate.net/publication/384780379_Integrating_Artificial_Intelligence_AI_in_Language_Teaching_Effectiveness_Challenges_and_Strategies

Meyer, A., Rose, D. H., & Gordon, D. (2014). *Universal design for learning: Theory and practice*. CAST Professional Publishing.

Nikula, T., Dalton-Puffer, C., Llinares, A., & Lorenzo, F. (2016). More than content and language: The complexity of integration in CLIL and bilingual education. In T. Nikula, E. Dafouz, P. Moore, & U. Smit (Eds.), *Conceptualising integration in CLIL and multilingual education* (pp. 1–26). Multilingual Matters.

Ooko, S. (2023). Digital literacy project improves learning in schools. *World Vision*. https://www.wvi.org/stories/kenya/digital-literacy-project-improves-learning-schools

Pane, J. F., Steiner, E. D., Baird, M. D., Hamilton, L. S., & Pane, J. D. (2017). *Informing progress: Insights on personalized learning implementation and effects*. RAND Corporation. https://www.rand.org/pubs/research_reports/RR2042.html

Paulsen, L., Dau, S., & Davidsen, J. (2024). Designing for collaborative learning in immersive virtual reality: A systematic literature review. *Virtual Reality, 28*(1), 63. https://link.springer.com/article/10.1007/s10055-024-00975-4

Pedaste, M., Mäeots, M., Siiman, L. A., De Jong, T., Van Riesen, S. A. N., Kamp, E. T., Manoli, C. C., Zacharia, Z. C., & Tsourlidaki, E. (2015). Phases of inquiry-based learning: Definitions and the inquiry cycle. *Educational Research*

Review, *14,* 47–61. https://www.sciencedirect.com/science/article/pii/ S1747938X15000068

Pretolesi, D., Zechner, O., Guirao, D. G., Schrom-Feiertag, H., & Tscheligi, M. (2023). AI-supported XR training: Personalizing medical first responder training. In *International conference on artificial intelligence and virtual reality* (pp. 343–356). Springer.

Walker, G., & Venker Weidenbenner, J. (2019). Social and emotional learning in the age of virtual play: Technology, empathy, and learning. *Journal of Research in Innovative Teaching & Learning, 12*(2), 116–132. https://www.emerald.com/insight/content/doi/10.1108/jrit-03-2019-0046/full/pdf?title=social-and-emotional-learning-in-the-age-of-virtual-play-technology-empathy-and-learning

Zhang, F., Zhang, Y., Li, G., & Luo, H. (2024). Using virtual reality interventions to promote social and emotional learning for children and adolescents: A systematic review and meta-analysis. *Children, 11*(1), 41. https://doi.org/10.3390/children11010041

CHAPTER 7

Conclusion: Shaping a DIGICOMPASS Future

Abstract This concluding chapter presents DIGICOMPASS as an evolving framework that reimagines twenty-first-century education through adaptive learning, immersive experiences, and cross-cultural collaboration. It underscores the irreplaceable role of teachers as mentors and facilitators, offering ethical guidance, emotional support, and contextual insights that technology alone cannot provide. At its core is the concept of the Global Classroom, which breaks down geographical and cultural barriers to enable real-time collaboration, shared learning, and the cultivation of plurilingual and intercultural competencies. The chapter concludes with key takeaways, reaffirming DIGICOMPASS's commitment to lifelong learning, inclusivity, and ethical engagement, empowering learners to confront global challenges with confidence, competence, and compassion.

Keywords Emergent technologies • Global Classroom • Lifelong learning • Professional growth • Teaching 2.0

7.1 Introduction

This final chapter crystallizes the essence of DIGICOMPASS not as an academic construct but as a dynamic, evolving framework designed to cultivate global citizenship. It articulates a vision of education that is proactive, creative, and responsible—qualities that define true global citizens capable of addressing the complex challenges of our world with knowledge, empathy, and decisive action. Naturally, a global citizen should be in a Global Classroom, as illustrated in Fig. 7.1, which depicts how ChatGPT 4.0 conceptualizes DIGICOMPASS fostering collaboration and engagement in a digitally connected, culturally diverse learning environment.

The Global Classroom envisions a learning environment that overcomes geographical and cultural divides, enabling students from diverse backgrounds to engage in real-time collaboration, problem-solving, and shared learning experiences. Even as education becomes increasingly digital, teachers remain central to the process. Their evolving roles as facilitators, mentors, and innovators ensure that education retains its deeply human character, fostering meaningful connections and guiding students through the complexities of a globalized world. After the discussion on Global Classrooms and the redefined roles of educators, DIGICOMPASS wraps up with key takeaways.

Fig. 7.1 DIGICOMPASS in a Global Classroom (as conceptualized by ChatGPT 4.0)

7.2 Envisioning a DIGICOMPASS Global Classroom

The concept of a Global Classroom represents a significant evolution in educational practices, where learning transcends geographical and cultural boundaries through the integration of digital technologies. In a Global Classroom, students from diverse parts of the world engage with each other in real-time, collaborate on projects, and participate in shared learning experiences. This concept aligns closely with the vision of the DIGICOMPASS framework, which emphasizes global citizenship, intercultural competence, and inclusive education. By fostering environments where students can interact across borders, the Global Classroom not only enhances academic learning but also prepares students to thrive in a diverse and interconnected world.

At its core, a Global Classroom is about creating opportunities for students to engage in meaningful, cross-cultural exchanges. It leverages digital tools like video conferencing, collaborative platforms, and social media to connect learners and educators from different countries, allowing them to share ideas, solve problems together, and gain insights from a variety of perspectives. This approach is particularly relevant to the DIGICOMPASS framework, which advocates for the development of global citizens who are well-versed in digital literacy and capable of navigating the complexities of a globalized society.

The integration of advanced technologies, such as AI and VR, further enhances the Global Classroom experience by creating immersive and personalized learning environments. As highlighted by Juarez et al. (2024), these technologies enable students to engage in projects that are not only collaborative but also deeply immersive, allowing them to experience different cultures and environments in a virtual space. This kind of learning experience aligns with the DIGICOMPASS vision by promoting intercultural understanding and cooperation, key components of global citizenship education.

Moreover, Lock (2015) underscores the importance of designing learning environments that actively engage students in global contexts. In a Global Classroom, educators are tasked with creating curricula that incorporate global perspectives and foster intercultural dialogue. This requires a careful selection of content that is relevant to students from diverse backgrounds and the inclusion of activities that encourage collaboration, such as group projects and virtual exchanges. The goal is to create a learning environment where students not only acquire academic knowledge but also develop the skills needed to engage with the world around them in meaningful ways.

A practical example of a Global Classroom in action is Khan Academy. This platform exemplifies how digital tools can be used to create a truly global learning environment. Khan Academy offers a vast library of educational content in multiple languages, making it accessible to students from all over the world. Through its platform, students can engage with the same learning materials, participate in global discussions, and collaborate with peers across different countries. This not only democratizes access to education but also fosters a global community of learners who can share their knowledge and experiences with each other. Khan Academy's role in the Global Classroom extends beyond just providing content. Its community features, such as discussion forums and peer-to-peer tutoring, allow students to interact with one another, ask questions, and receive feedback, regardless of their location. This kind of interaction is crucial for building the intercultural competence that the DIGICOMPASS framework advocates. By participating in these global learning communities, students can develop a deeper understanding of different cultures and perspectives, which is essential for their growth as global citizens.

Setting up a Global Classroom involves several key steps, each of which is crucial for creating an environment conducive to international collaboration and learning. First, it requires a robust technology infrastructure that includes high-speed Internet, access to collaborative platforms like Google Workspace or Microsoft Teams, and tools for virtual communication such as Zoom or Skype. These platforms facilitate real-time interaction between students and educators across different time zones and geographical locations, making the classroom truly global.

The curriculum design also plays a vital role in the success of a Global Classroom. Educators must design curricula that incorporate global perspectives and promote intercultural dialogue. This includes selecting content that is relevant to students from diverse backgrounds and integrating activities that encourage collaboration, such as group projects, virtual exchanges, and online discussions. By doing so, educators can create a learning environment that is not only academically rigorous but also culturally enriching.

Moreover, the use of advanced technologies like AI and VR can significantly enhance the Global Classroom experience. As Juarez et al. (2024) point out, these technologies can create immersive learning environments where students can collaborate on projects, solve problems, and develop competencies in a multicultural setting. AI can be used to tailor learning experiences to individual students, while VR can create simulations that allow students to explore different cultures and environments in a virtual space.

Establishing partnerships with schools and institutions in different countries is another crucial step in setting up a Global Classroom. These partnerships enable the exchange of ideas, resources, and best practices, ensuring that the classroom remains truly global. Programs like Khan Academy, which offer content in multiple languages and are accessible worldwide, exemplify how global education can be democratized and made available to a broad audience.

Finally, teacher training and support are essential for the successful implementation of a Global Classroom. Educators must be equipped with the skills and knowledge to effectively manage and facilitate a Global Classroom. This involves professional development opportunities that focus on digital literacy, intercultural communication, and the use of advanced technologies in education. As O'Dowd (2018) emphasizes, teachers play a crucial role in guiding students through the complexities of global learning, ensuring that the experience is both educational and culturally enriching.

In conclusion, the Global Classroom is not just a theoretical concept but a practical, necessary innovation for twenty-first-century education. By leveraging digital tools, designing inclusive curricula, and integrating advanced technologies like AI and VR, educators can create learning environments that transcend borders. The Global Classroom represents the future of education—one where learning is collaborative, culturally aware, and accessible to all, regardless of location. This aligns seamlessly with the DIGICOMPASS framework, which advocates for the development of global citizens who are equipped to navigate the challenges and opportunities of an interconnected world. However, the success of the Global Classroom hinges not just on the technology itself but on how educators adapt and evolve their roles within this new paradigm. As we move towards a more interconnected and technologically driven educational landscape, the concept of "Teaching 2.0" emerges (Fig. 7.2), highlighting the critical need to redefine the roles of teachers in this digital age.

Fig. 7.2 Teaching 2.0 in the age of emerging technologies

7.3 Redefining Teacher Roles in the Age of Emerging Technologies

The advent of emerging technologies like AI and XR has dramatically transformed the educational landscape, providing tools that can personalize learning, enhance engagement, and create immersive experiences. These technologies, however, far from rendering teachers obsolete, highlight the indispensable role that educators play in the learning process. While AI and XR offer unprecedented opportunities, they lack the nuanced understanding, ethical guidance, and emotional support that only human teachers can provide. This discussion explores the irreplaceable roles of teachers and why, no matter how advanced technology becomes, it will never fully replace the human touch in education.

One of the most significant advancements in educational technology is AI's ability to analyze vast amounts of data to tailor learning experiences to individual students. Adaptive learning platforms can identify students' strengths and weaknesses, adjusting the difficulty of tasks to suit their needs. However, the true value of personalized learning lies not just in the data, but in the interpretation and application of these AI-driven insights, a task that requires a deep understanding of human educators (Nguyen et al., 2023). According to Yan (2023), the role of teachers is evolving rather than diminishing; educators are now tasked with integrating technological insights into a holistic understanding of each student. Teachers see beyond data points, understanding the emotional, social, and cognitive aspects of their students' learning. For instance, a teacher might notice a student's anxiety, boredom, or disengagement—factors that AI might not detect—and adjust their approach accordingly. This ability to understand and respond to the nuanced needs of students ensures that education remains a personalized and human-centered process, despite the increasing presence of AI (Akgun & Greenhow, 2022).

Furthermore, XR, including VR and AR, offers immersive environments that make learning more engaging and interactive. These technologies can transport students to different times, places, and cultures, providing experiences that would be impossible in a traditional classroom. However, the effectiveness of these immersive experiences depends heavily on the guidance of a teacher (Holmes & Littlejohn, 2024). Yan (2023) emphasizes that as educational technologies become more advanced, the role of the teacher becomes even more crucial in contextualizing and guiding these experiences. Teachers ensure that students not only engage with the content but also understand and learn from it. For example, a language teacher using VR to simulate cultural immersion must provide context, facilitate discussions, and help students connect these virtual experiences to their language learning goals. Without the teacher's involvement, these technologies risk becoming mere entertainment rather than powerful educational tools. The teacher's role in bridging the gap between immersive experiences and educational outcomes is thus irreplaceable (Georgieva et al., 2024).

In addition to guiding learning, one of the most profound roles of teachers in the digital age is providing ethical and cultural guidance. AI and XR technologies introduce significant ethical and cultural considerations, particularly in how data is used, how immersive experiences are designed, and how these tools impact society. Teachers are essential in navigating these complexities, helping students critically evaluate the technologies they use and understand their broader implications (Nguyen et al., 2023). Yan (2023) argues that the evolving role of the teacher includes being a moral compass in the classroom, guiding students through the ethical dilemmas posed by emerging technologies. Teachers facilitate discussions about the ethical implications of AI, such as privacy concerns, bias in algorithms, and the societal impact of automation. They also provide cultural context, helping students understand and appreciate the diverse perspectives that these technologies can introduce. This human-centered approach is crucial for developing students' critical thinking skills and preparing them to navigate a technologically advanced world with a deep understanding of ethical and cultural nuances (Akgun & Greenhow, 2022).

Beyond these cognitive and ethical roles, teachers provide emotional support and mentorship, which are critical components of a positive learning environment. While AI can offer personalized feedback and XR can create engaging experiences, neither can replace the relationships that teachers build with their students. Teachers understand their students' emotional needs, offering encouragement, empathy, and support that technology cannot replicate. They help students navigate the social and psychological challenges of learning, fostering resilience, self-confidence, and a love of learning. This emotional connection is essential for maintaining student engagement and motivation, particularly in challenging or stressful learning situations. Teachers' ability to provide this level of emotional support makes them indispensable, regardless of technological advancements (Akgun & Greenhow, 2022).

As technology evolves, so too must the role of the teacher. Continuous professional development is essential for educators to stay updated on the latest technological advancements and to integrate these tools effectively into their teaching practices. Teachers who embrace ongoing learning can use AI and XR to enhance their instruction, ensuring that their teaching remains relevant and impactful (Holmes & Littlejohn, 2024). Yan (2023) highlights that the modern teacher must be an innovator, constantly evolving alongside technology to effectively meet the needs of their students. This commitment to professional growth underscores the dynamic nature of teaching, where educators are not just users of technology but also innovators who can creatively leverage these tools to benefit their students. The teacher's role in guiding technological integration, rather than being replaced by it, is crucial for the future of education (Georgieva et al., 2024).

While AI and XR offer remarkable capabilities, there are aspects of teaching that technology will never be able to replicate. First and foremost, teachers possess the ability to understand and respond to the complexities of human emotions, something that even the most advanced AI cannot do. The empathy, intuition, and personal connection that teachers bring to their interactions with students are irreplaceable (Holmes & Littlejohn, 2024). Additionally, teachers provide ethical and cultural guidance that requires a deep understanding of human society, history, and values. This type of guidance is essential for developing well-rounded, critically thinking individuals who can navigate the moral and societal challenges of a technologically advanced world. Finally, teachers foster relationships that are built on trust, understanding, and mutual respect—relationships that are fundamental to the learning process and that technology will never be able to replicate (Yan, 2023).

In sum, emerging technologies like AI and XR are transforming education, offering tools that enhance personalized learning, engagement, and immersive experiences. However, these technologies do not replace the critical roles that teachers play. Educators are indispensable in interpreting data, providing ethical and cultural context, and offering the emotional support necessary for meaningful and effective learning experiences. The human touch that teachers bring to education is irreplaceable, ensuring that technology serves to complement and enhance the educational process rather than replace it. No matter how advanced technology becomes, the role of the teacher as a guide, mentor, and human connection in the learning journey will always remain essential.

7.4 DIGICOMPASS Wrap-up and Takeaways

As we conclude, it is essential to revisit the core principles and innovations that define DIGICOMPASS. This comprehensive, forward-looking framework is designed to navigate the complexities of contemporary education and global citizenship by harmonizing emergent technologies, personalized learning, and a deep commitment to inclusivity and ethical practices. The ten key takeaways encapsulate the essence of the DIGICOMPASS framework:

John Dewey, a pioneering figure in education and a key proponent of Constructivism—a theoretical underpinning of DIGICOMPASS—once said, "Education is not preparation for life; education is life itself." DIGICOMPASS embodies this philosophy, equipping students with the tools they need not only to succeed but to lead in a world that is

1. **Core Principles**: DIGICOMPASS is built upon four cardinal points—digital literacy, inclusive practices, intercultural competence, and awareness of social strategies. These principles are not just theoretical; they form a cohesive approach that prepares students to navigate the modern world with confidence and competence.
2. **Digital Literacy as a Foundation**: Serving as the "North" of the metaphorical compass, digital literacy is a foundational element that emphasizes not only technical skills but also critical thinking, ethical engagement, and active participation in digital communities. It is the bedrock upon which all other literacies and multiliteracies within the framework are built.
3. **Integration of Emergent Technologies**: DIGICOMPASS is at the forefront of educational innovation, integrating technologies like artificial intelligence (AI), extended reality (XR), and adaptive learning. These tools create personalized, inclusive, and immersive learning environments that cater to diverse student needs, ensuring they are well-prepared for the digital future.
4. **Personalized and Inclusive Learning**: The framework ensures that education is tailored to individual needs through adaptive learning technologies and assistive tools, providing an inclusive educational experience that is accessible to all students, regardless of their backgrounds.
5. **Intercultural and Plurilingual Competence**: In an increasingly globalized world, the ability to navigate multiple languages and cultures is crucial. DIGICOMPASS prioritizes intercultural competence and plurilingualism, equipping students with the skills necessary for effective communication and collaboration across diverse cultural contexts.
6. **Global Integration and Classroom Concept**: DIGICOMPASS aligns seamlessly with national and international educational standards, making it adaptable across various educational systems worldwide. The "Global Classroom" concept exemplifies the framework's commitment to fostering global citizenship and intercultural competence through digital platforms.

(continued)

(continued)

7. **Redefining Teacher Roles**: In the digital age, teachers are more critical than ever. DIGICOMPASS emphasizes the evolving role of educators as providers of ethical guidance, cultural context, and emotional support—roles that technology alone cannot replace. Continuous professional development is vital to equip educators for these evolving responsibilities.
8. **Experiential Learning**: DIGICOMPASS supports experiential learning approaches such as project-based learning (PBL), inquiry-based learning (IBL), scenario-based learning (SBL), and content and language integrated learning (CLIL). Enhanced by AI and XR technologies, these methods allow students to engage in personalized, hands-on activities that are both relevant and adaptive.
9. **Continuous Formative Assessment**: AI and XR technologies enable continuous formative assessment within DIGICOMPASS, providing real-time insights into student performance and allowing educators to make dynamic instructional adjustments, ensuring that learning is always aligned with student needs.
10. **Commitment to Inclusivity, Sustainability, and Global Citizenship**: DIGICOMPASS is deeply committed to inclusivity, bridging educational disparities and ensuring access to high-quality education for all students. The framework also weaves sustainability and ethical practices throughout the curriculum, preparing students to be responsible global citizens who can address societal and environmental challenges.

increasingly interconnected and digital. Dewey's Constructivist ideals resonate throughout the framework, emphasizing active learning, social interaction, and the continuous development of knowledge. As we look ahead, DIGICOMPASS will continue to serve as a guiding force, helping educators and students alike navigate the challenges and opportunities of the future with confidence, competence, and compassion.

References

Akgun, S., & Greenhow, C. (2022). Artificial intelligence in education: Addressing ethical challenges in K-12 settings. *AI and Ethics, 2*(3), 431–440. https://link.springer.com/article/10.1007/s43681-021-00096-7

Georgieva, M., Nelson, J., LaFosse, R., & Contis, D. (2024). Navigating the XR educational landscape: Privacy, safety, and ethical guidelines. *EDUCAUSE*. https://www.educause.edu/research/community/2024/navigating-the-xr-educational-landscape-privacy-safety-and-ethical-guidelines/introduction

Holmes, W., & Littlejohn, A. (2024). Artificial intelligence for professional learning. In M. Garcia-Murillo, I. MacInnes, & A. Renda (Eds.), *Handbook of artificial intelligence at work: Interconnections and policy implications* (pp. 191–211). Edward Elgar Publishing.

Juarez, A., Rabago, J., Pliego, L., Salazar, G., & Gonzalez, P. (2024). Integrating AI and VR in global classroom: Enhancing design competencies through multicultural collaboration. In *EDULEARN24 Proceedings* (pp. 89–97). IATED Digital Library.

Lock, J. V. (2015). Designing learning to engage students in the global classroom. *Technology, Pedagogy and Education, 24*(2), 137–153.

Nguyen, A., Ngo, H. N., Hong, Y., Dang, B., & Nguyen, B. P. T. (2023). Ethical principles for artificial intelligence in education. *Education and Information Technologies, 28*(4), 4221–4241. https://link.springer.com/article/10.1007/s10639-022-11316-w

O'Dowd, R. (2018). From telecollaboration to virtual exchange: State-of-the-art and the role of UNICollaboration in moving forward. *Journal of Virtual Exchange, 1*, 1–23. https://doi.org/10.14705/rpnet.2018.jve.1

Yan, S. (2023). From tradition to modernity: Redefining the role of the teacher in the 21st century. In *Proceedings of ICEMEET 2023*. Francis Academic Press. https://webofproceedings.org/proceedings_series/ECOM/ICEMEET%202023/EM003.pdf

Index[1]

A
Abilities, 3, 14, 18, 45, 50, 60, 61, 66, 67, 74, 76, 83, 89, 105, 117, 118, 136, 139, 153
Accessibility, 48, 52, 61–63, 65, 98, 104, 117, 124, 130, 138
Accessible, 16, 25, 31, 33, 35, 47, 48, 50–53, 58, 61, 66, 67, 122–124, 141, 150, 152
Adaptive, 14, 15, 25–28, 30, 31, 44–48, 52, 54, 56, 59–64, 67
Adaptive learning technologies, 6, 14, 15, 25–31, 44, 46, 47, 52, 59–62, 64, 67, 117, 119, 127, 136, 140, 141, 160, 166, 169, 178
Adaptive technologies, 5
Adaptivity, 17
Advanced technologies, 9
AI-XR, 140, 156
Algorithms, 27, 29, 30, 46, 52, 53, 58–60, 140, 144, 180

Analytic, 44, 50, 53, 67
Approach, 12, 14–16, 18, 19, 21–25, 30–32, 34
Artificial intelligence (AI), 5, 26–31, 46, 52, 56–62, 64–67, 115, 119, 127, 136, 140–158, 160, 169, 175–181
Assessment, 8, 52, 53, 65, 67, 98, 110, 112, 113, 118–121, 124, 136, 163, 167–169
Assistive, 31, 44, 48, 52, 54, 60, 62–64, 66, 67, 117, 123, 130
Augmented reality (AR), 49, 52, 56–59, 63, 144, 145, 147
Automatic Speech Recognition, 27
Awareness of social strategies, 13, 18, 19, 78, 102

B
Blended learning, 58

---

[1] Note: Page numbers followed by 'n' refer to notes.

C

Cognitive load theory, 44, 45, 48, 50, 60, 80, 104, 139
Collaboration, 6, 14, 25, 30, 51, 53–55, 59, 64, 66, 89, 90, 104, 113, 128, 129, 139, 157, 174–176
Collaborative, 44–46, 48, 49, 52–55, 57, 59, 60, 63, 64, 66, 67, 80, 82, 84, 85, 104, 107, 116, 117, 125–128, 139, 168, 175–177
Collective, 12, 107, 116, 128
Common European Framework of Reference for Languages (CEFR), 18, 22–25, 87, 99, 104–110, 161–163, 167–169
Communication, 2, 5, 6, 14, 16, 18, 22–26, 31, 46, 48, 49, 53–56, 66, 67, 74–78, 80, 82–85, 87–89, 91, 101, 104–110, 125, 154, 155, 158, 162, 163, 165, 166, 176, 177
Communicative, 21, 23, 24, 56, 80, 87, 105, 106, 108, 109, 139
Community, 19
Compass, 9, 12, 13, 179
Competencies, 5, 74, 78, 80, 84, 86–90, 99, 106, 111–113, 115, 127, 130, 153, 155, 158
Computer-assisted language learning, 57
Connectivism, 44, 45, 48, 50, 60, 80, 104, 139
Connectivist, 139
Connectivity, 45, 80, 122
Constructivism, 44–46, 52, 59, 80, 104, 139, 181
Constructivist, 138
Content and Language Integrated Learning (CLIL), 21, 139, 143, 148–150, 155, 156, 158
Content delivery, 29, 31, 44, 50, 53, 60, 64, 66, 67, 148
Core principles, 7–9, 13–19
Creative and innovative multiliteracy, 85
Critical literacy, 103
Critical thinking, 14, 19, 22, 32, 74, 76, 77, 81–85, 88, 89, 91, 101, 104, 107, 116, 120, 139, 147, 157, 159, 180
Cross-cultural, 18, 26, 33, 104, 175
Cultural awareness, 5, 148, 150, 151, 158
Cultural competence, 140, 151, 152
Cultural literacy, 103
Culturally responsive education (CRE), 16, 17, 150–152, 156, 158, 160, 169
Culture, 3, 6
Curriculum, 4, 16, 17, 19, 24, 25, 33, 34, 52, 59, 98, 99, 101, 104–106, 110–122, 124–126, 128, 129, 151, 152, 156, 160

D

Data analytics, 28–30, 50, 52, 53, 57, 64–66, 118, 120, 121, 140, 169
Developmental Model of Intercultural Sensitivity, 17
Differentiated instruction, 14, 15, 119, 136
Differentiation, 15, 17
DIGICOMPASS, 2–9, 12–25, 12n1, 27, 30–35, 44–55, 59, 60, 62–64, 67, 74, 78–91, 98, 99, 101–123, 125–128, 130, 136–169, 174–177, 181–183
DIGICOMPASS Future, 8
Digital, 4, 8, 9, 13–15, 19, 25–27, 31, 33, 35, 45, 47–49, 52, 54, 56–58, 60, 61, 63, 67, 74–78,

80–86, 88–91, 98, 99, 101–104, 106, 107, 111, 112, 114, 116–119, 122–128, 130, 139, 140, 143, 152, 154–156, 158, 164–169, 174–177, 179, 183
Digital literacy, 3–5, 8, 9, 13–14, 19, 31, 33, 45, 61, 74, 77–78, 81, 86, 90, 91, 98, 99, 101–104, 106, 114, 122, 123, 126, 127, 143, 152, 155, 156, 164, 175, 177
Digital multiliteracy, 85
Digital storytelling, 13, 89, 104, 158–160, 163–169
Diverse, 7, 14–17, 21, 22, 25, 26, 28, 32, 33, 45, 50, 58, 60–62, 66, 74, 76, 78, 80, 84, 86, 88–91, 98, 99, 101, 105–108, 110, 111, 115, 117, 120–122, 124–126, 128, 130, 136, 139, 140, 150–152, 154, 158, 159, 169, 174–176, 180
Diversity, 18, 22, 81, 88, 99, 105, 124, 140

E

Ecological approach, 55
Education, 1, 3–9, 12, 14, 16, 18, 19, 21–24, 26–28, 30, 31, 33–35, 44, 58, 60–62, 67, 76, 77, 81–84, 86–91, 98, 99, 104, 111, 114, 115, 125, 130, 140, 150, 152, 158, 169, 174–181
Embodied cognition, 55
Emergent technologies, 5–6
Engagement, 14–19, 26–28, 30, 31, 33, 35, 49–52, 54, 57–64, 66, 67, 74, 78, 81, 84, 85, 91, 99, 101, 106, 110, 112, 115, 117, 120, 121, 123–125, 127, 130, 140, 143, 144, 147–152, 158, 159, 164, 167, 178, 180, 181
Equitable, 5, 7, 14, 21, 26, 33, 58, 61, 66, 76, 77, 81, 90, 104, 123, 130, 150, 151
Equity, 7, 8, 104, 114, 126
Ethical, 8, 14, 18, 19, 31–35, 74, 77, 81, 82, 84–86, 91, 99, 104, 121, 130, 154, 156, 169, 178–181
Ethical and critical multiliteracy, 84
Ethical engagement, 9
Ethical literacy, 103
Evaluation, 5, 118, 120, 121
Experiential, 48, 49, 52, 63, 67, 138, 139, 143, 148, 151, 155–157, 169
Experiential learning, 101, 115, 137, 138, 140, 143–151, 155–158, 169
Extended reality (XR), 49, 57–59, 63, 66, 67, 136, 140–158, 169, 178–181

F

Feedback, 26–30, 47, 50, 53, 54, 56, 60–62, 65, 67, 98, 110–114, 116, 118–121, 125, 127–129, 136, 140, 141, 143–149, 154–156, 167, 168, 176, 180
Financial and economic multiliteracy, 84
Framework, 3–9, 12–14, 16–18, 21–24, 26, 28, 31–35, 44, 45, 52, 55, 59, 60, 62, 67, 74, 76, 80, 81, 86–89, 91, 98, 99, 102, 104, 106, 110, 111, 115–118, 124, 127, 130, 136, 140, 150, 152, 153, 155–158, 169, 174–177, 181, 183

G

Gamification, 6, 44, 50, 51, 53, 54, 62, 64, 66, 67
Global, 13, 14, 16, 17, 19, 21, 23, 25, 26, 32–35, 74, 76–78, 80, 83–86, 88–91, 98, 99, 101, 102, 104, 106, 110, 111, 124, 130, 136, 139, 140, 149, 151, 152, 156–158, 160
Global and environmental multiliteracy, 84
Global citizen, 174
Global citizenship, 2, 12, 14, 19, 23, 32–35, 74, 78, 84, 85, 88–91, 98, 102, 104, 106, 111, 130, 136, 140, 151, 152, 174–177, 181
Global classroom, 174–177
Global language education, 3, 4, 6, 8, 9, 19, 99

H

Holistic, 3, 12, 18, 44, 59, 87, 102, 115, 116, 118, 136–158, 179
Human rights and advocacy multiliteracy, 84

I

Immersion, 6
Immersive, 8, 44, 48, 49, 52–54, 56–59, 62–64, 66, 67, 117, 141, 143, 145, 147–152, 154–156, 164, 165, 169, 175, 176, 178, 179, 181
Inclusion, 8
Inclusive, 6, 13, 15–17, 19, 21, 25, 26, 33, 44, 46, 52, 58, 61, 62, 66, 67, 76, 81, 87, 102, 104–107, 111, 115, 117, 122, 130, 136, 138, 139, 150, 151, 156–158, 169, 175, 177
Inclusive practices, 13–17, 19, 21, 78, 102, 104–106, 115, 138, 150–156, 159–160
Inclusivity, 14, 48, 52, 61, 63, 67, 105, 110, 111, 117, 124, 130, 169
Innovation literacy, 103
Input, 27, 28, 52, 54–57, 60, 141
Input hypothesis, 54
Inquiry, 139, 143, 147, 148, 158
Inquiry-based learning, 139, 143, 146–148, 155, 158, 169
Integration, 9
Intelligent tutoring systems, 27, 56
Interaction, 14, 17, 22, 25, 45, 49, 52–57, 59, 80, 81, 86, 88, 99, 105–107, 109, 119, 120, 128, 139, 145, 147–149, 151, 154, 155, 162, 181
Interaction hypothesis, 54
Interactionist approach, 54–56, 59
Interactive, 28, 46, 48–54, 56–59, 61, 63, 64, 66, 67, 74, 76, 77, 84, 86, 91, 106, 109, 112, 117–119, 124, 128, 139, 144, 145, 148, 156, 159, 162, 164–166
Interconnected, 17, 24, 25, 32, 35, 66, 67, 74, 77, 86, 89, 99, 111, 156, 175, 177, 183
Interconnectedness, 34, 55, 77, 89
Intercultural, 7, 17–19, 21–25, 32, 80, 82, 84, 86–89, 98, 99, 101, 102, 105–108, 148, 156, 159, 175–177
Intercultural and plurilingual multiliteracy, 84, 86–89
Intercultural communication, 17, 18, 21, 23, 24
Intercultural competence, 3–5, 13, 17–19, 21, 22, 24, 25, 47, 53, 58, 78, 98, 99, 102, 105, 106, 148, 156, 159, 175, 176
Intercultural literacy, 103, 106

INDEX   189

Intercultural understanding, 2, 21, 22
Interdisciplinary, 4, 6, 106, 111, 113, 115, 116, 128
Interdisciplinary learning, 3
International Baccalaureate, 99, 101

L

Language education, 2, 3, 5, 6, 19, 21, 23–27, 33, 35, 54, 58, 99, 106, 111
Language learning, 18, 21–24, 47, 54–59, 82, 85–88, 139, 149, 158
Learners, 6, 7, 9
Learning, 3–7
Learning environment, 3, 8, 14, 16, 25–30, 44–48, 52, 53, 58, 59, 61–64, 66, 67, 104, 111, 115, 116, 123, 138, 140, 141, 145, 147, 150, 152, 154, 155, 158, 175–177, 180
Learning outcomes, 15, 28, 30, 61, 62, 66, 81, 102, 118, 120, 121, 127
Learning pathways, 3, 5
Lifelong learning, 33, 156
Literacy, 13, 74–78, 81, 83, 84, 86, 88–91
Local, 21, 32, 34, 98, 101, 102, 110–112, 117, 125, 126, 129, 151

M

Media literacy, 91
Mediation, 104–107, 162
Mixed-methods assessments, 118, 122
Mixed reality (MR), 49, 52, 57, 63
Mobile-assisted language learning, 59
Mobility, 33, 34
Modular, 3, 4, 12, 106, 112, 115, 127, 128

Module, 24, 29, 110, 111, 113, 117, 121, 136, 158–160, 164
Multicultural, 8, 58, 86, 88, 89, 101, 177
Multilingual, 82, 87, 88, 106, 108, 124, 158, 162
Multilingualism, 57, 58
Multiliteracies, 8, 13, 25, 74, 76, 78, 80, 81, 84, 85, 88–91, 156, 160–161
Multimedia, 51, 76, 84, 86, 90, 112, 117, 119, 128, 159, 164, 168
Multimodality, 55

N

National educational standards, 98, 99
Natural language processing (NLP), 27–30, 154

O

Online, 45, 47, 53, 61, 64, 74, 77, 78, 81, 82, 85, 86, 118, 119, 128, 176
Output, 28, 29, 56, 57
Output hypothesis, 54

P

Personalization, 17, 29–31, 45, 46, 61
Personalized learning, 5, 9, 14, 15, 27, 28, 30, 31, 44, 45, 47, 56, 57, 59–61, 64, 67, 119, 136, 140–143, 145, 148, 160–161, 166, 175, 179, 181
Pluricultural competence, 87, 99, 106, 158, 162
Plurilingual, 21, 22, 25, 58, 86–89, 91, 99, 105, 106, 108, 148, 158, 162
Plurilingualism, 19, 25, 54, 56–59, 87, 88, 103, 105

Plurilingual Literacy, 103
Pragmatic competence, 22, 25, 99, 105, 106, 163
Processing, 28, 29
Professional development, 98, 114–117, 126, 127, 130, 177, 180
Professional learning communities, 116, 117, 127, 128
Project-based learning, 19, 32, 33, 101, 139, 143, 145, 146, 148, 155, 158, 169

R
Reality, 5
Reflective practice, 19, 116, 143, 144, 146
Research mentorship, 116, 117
Resource allocation, 15
Resource development, 112, 115–117, 128
Resources, 101, 110, 112, 114, 115, 117, 119, 122–126, 128, 129

S
Scaffolding, 45, 48, 139, 148
Scalability, 98, 111, 114, 115
Scenario-based learning, 138, 139, 143–145, 147, 148, 155, 158, 159, 169
Science, 3
Second language acquisition (SLA), 54, 56, 59
Service learning, 32, 104, 145, 146
Signing competence, 105, 106
Skills, 2, 6, 9, 13, 14, 16–19, 22–27, 31, 33, 47, 57, 61, 66, 67, 74, 76–78, 82, 83, 85–91, 101, 102, 104–109, 115, 118, 120, 123, 139, 143, 148–150, 153–155, 158, 164, 168, 176, 177, 180

Social awareness, 16
Social entrepreneurship, 19
Social literacy, 103
Social media, 14, 76, 175
Social responsibility, 18, 19, 32–35, 99, 104
Social studies, 3
Social-emotional learning (SEL), 16, 17, 150, 153–156, 158, 159
Sociocultural Theory, 44, 45, 48, 54, 55, 60, 80, 104, 139
Sociolinguistic competence, 22, 25, 99, 106, 109
Speech production, 27
Speech recognition, 27
Strategic implementation, 98, 106–117
Strategies, 14, 15, 17–19, 21–23, 25, 32, 44, 60, 64, 66, 67, 98, 102, 107, 108, 111, 113, 115–119, 121, 122, 126–128, 130, 136, 140, 143, 154, 157
Students, 2, 3, 5–9, 13–19, 21, 23–26, 30–35, 45, 47–58, 60, 61, 63–67, 74–77, 80, 81, 84–91, 99, 101, 104–107, 109–111, 113, 115–126, 130, 136, 138–141, 143–156, 158–160, 164, 165, 167, 174–181
Sustainability, 16, 28, 32, 34, 111, 130, 156, 159
Sustainable, 14, 19, 27, 32–34, 104, 130

T
Teacher education, 8
Teacher research, 116
Teachers, 4, 16, 26, 31, 45, 48, 53, 56, 58, 66, 102, 110, 113, 114, 116, 120, 123, 124, 126–129, 174, 177–181
Teacher training, 15, 115, 177

Technology, 1, 3, 5–8, 27, 31, 44, 45, 47, 50, 58–60, 110, 114, 117, 118, 120, 122–123, 125–127, 130, 136, 139, 140, 143, 152, 157, 164, 176–178, 180, 181
Text-to-Speech, 27
Translanguaging, 24, 55, 56, 87
21st-century, 136, 157, 177

U

Understanding, 5–7, 9, 12–15, 17, 18, 21–26, 31–35, 44, 47–49, 53–55, 58, 61, 65–67, 74, 76–78, 80–91, 99, 101, 104, 105, 107, 108, 116, 118, 119, 139, 141, 143–150, 154, 158–161, 165, 167, 175, 176, 178–181

UNESCO, 14, 77, 90
UNICEF, 32
United Nations Sustainable Development Goals (UN SDGs), 33, 99, 102, 103
Universal Design for Learning (UDL), 16, 17, 150, 152, 156, 158, 159, 169
Usage-based theories, 55

V

Virtual, 45, 49, 52, 57, 63, 144, 145, 149, 151, 155, 175–177, 179
Virtual Reality (VR), 49, 52, 56–59, 63, 141, 144, 145, 147, 149, 151, 154–156, 158, 160, 164–166, 175–177, 179

The manufacturer's authorised representative in the EU is Springer Nature Customer Service Centre GmbH, Europaplatz 3, 69115 Heidelberg, Germany. If you have any concerns regarding our products, please contact ProductSafety@springernature.com

Printed and bound by CPI Group (UK) Ltd, Croydon, CR0 4YY
17/07/2025
01918353-0001